Book and CD for B♭, E♭, C and Bass Clef Instruments

BIG JAZZ STANDARDS COLLECTION

volume 118

20 GREAT CLASSICS

Arranged and Produced by
Mark Taylor and Jim Roberts

BOOK

ISBN 978-1-4234-8544-5

7777 W. Bluemound Rd. P.O. Box 13819 Milwaukee, WI 53213

Visit Hal Leonard Online at
www.halleonard.com

CDs

TITLE	CD Track Number Split Track/Melody	CD Track Number Full Stereo Track
CD1		
All the Things You Are	1	2
Almost Like Being in Love	3	4
Blue Skies	5	6
Can't Help Lovin' Dat Man	7	8
Come Rain or Come Shine	9	10
Desafinado	11	12
Don't Get Around Much Anymore	13	14
For All We Know	15	16
I Gotta Right to Sing the Blues	17	18
I Wish I Didn't Love You So	19	20
B♭ Tuning Notes		21
CD2		
I'll Take Romance	1	2
In the Wee Small Hours of the Morning	3	4
Just in Time	5	6
Like Someone in Love	7	8
Lollipops and Roses	9	10
Love Is Just Around the Corner	11	12
My Ideal	13	14
On a Slow Boat to China	15	16
Too Late Now	17	18
You Are Too Beautiful	19	20
B♭ Tuning Notes		21

BIG JAZZ STANDARDS COLLECTION

Volume 118

Arranged and Produced by
Mark Taylor and Jim Roberts

Featured Players:

Graham Breedlove–Trumpet and Flugelhorn
John Desalme–Tenor Saxophone
Tony Nalker–Piano
Jim Roberts–Bass
Todd Harrison–Drums
Steve Fidyk–Drums

Recorded at Bias Studios, Springfield, Virginia
Bob Dawson, Engineer

HOW TO USE THE CD:

Each song has two tracks:

1) Split Track/Melody

Woodwind, Brass, Keyboard, and **Mallet Players** can use this track as a learning tool for melody style and inflection.

Bass Players can learn and perform with this track – remove the recorded bass track by turning down the volume on the LEFT channel.

Keyboard and **Guitar Players** can learn and perform with this track – remove the recorded piano part by turning down the volume on the RIGHT channel.

2) Full Stereo Track

Soloists or **Groups** can learn and perform with this accompaniment track with the RHYTHM SECTION only.

CD #1

❶ : SPLIT TRACK/MELODY

❷ : FULL STEREO TRACK

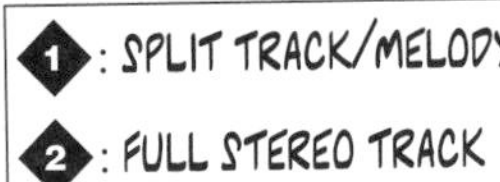

ALL THE THINGS YOU ARE

FROM VERY WARM FOR MAY

LYRICS BY OSCAR HAMMERSTEIN II
MUSIC BY JEROME KERN

C VERSION

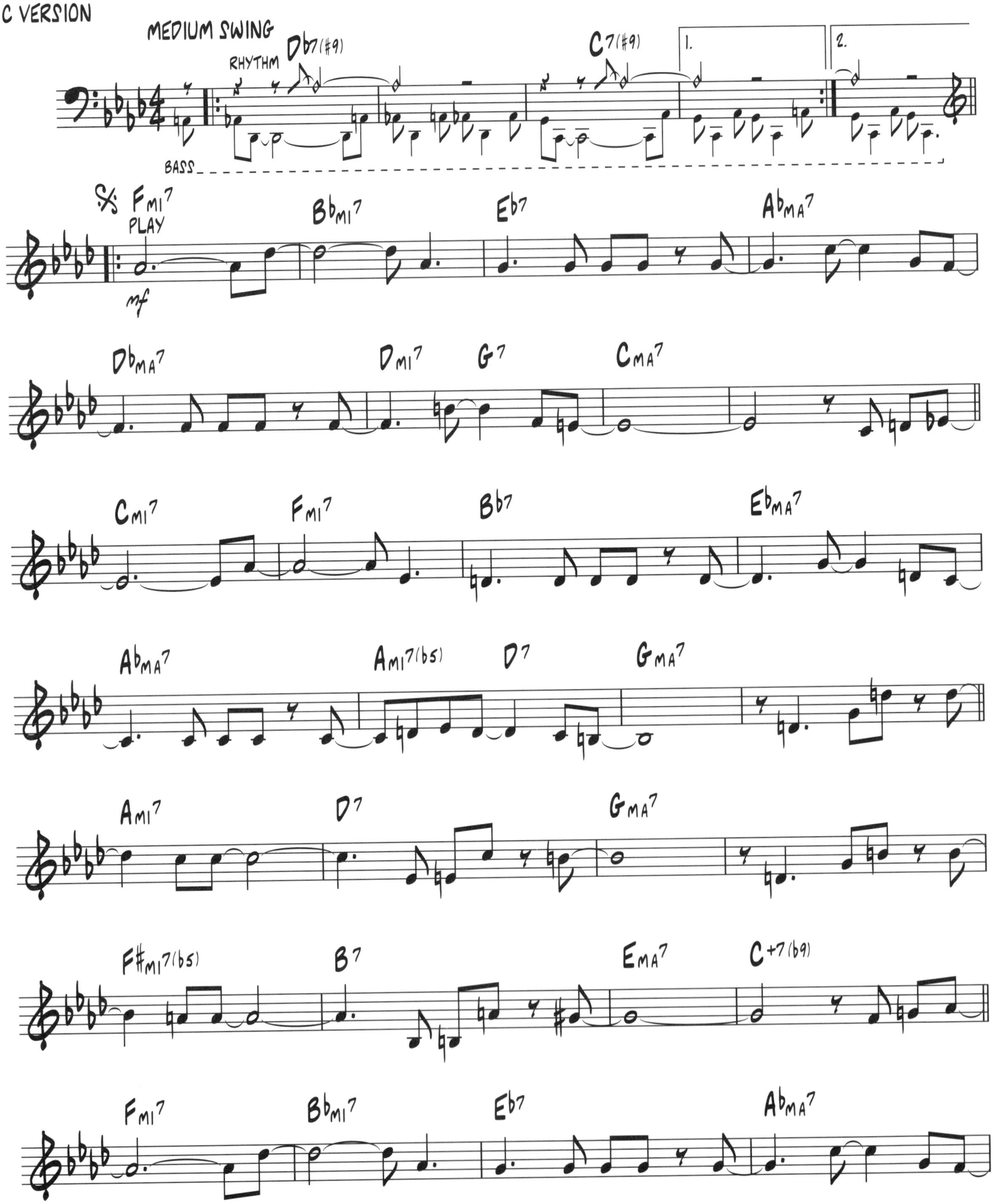
MEDIUM SWING
RHYTHM
Db7(#9)
C7(#9)
1.
2.
BASS
Fmi7
PLAY
mf
Bbmi7
Eb7
Abma7
Dbma7
Dmi7
G7
Cma7
Cmi7
Fmi7
Bb7
Ebma7
Abma7
Ami7(b5)
D7
Gma7
Ami7
D7
Gma7
F#mi7(b5)
B7
Ema7
C+7(b9)
Fmi7
Bbmi7
Eb7
Abma7

Dbma7
Gb7
Cmi7
B°7
Bbmi7
Eb7
TO CODA
Ab6
Gmi7(b5) C7(b9)
SOLOS (2 CHORUSES)
Fmi7
Bbmi7
Eb7
Abma7
Dbma7
Dmi7 G7
Cma7
Cmi7
Fmi7
Bb7
Ebma7
Abma7
Ami7(b5) D7
Gma7
Ami7
D7
Gma7
F#mi7(b5)
B7
Ema7
C+7(b9)
Fmi7
Bbmi7
Eb7
Abma7
Dbma7
Gb7
Cmi7
B°7
Bbmi7
Eb7
Ab6
D.S. AL CODA
Gmi7(b5) C7(b9)
CODA
N.C.
Db7(#9)
1ST X ONLY
1.
C7(#9)
2.
C7(#9)

CD #1

3 : SPLIT TRACK/MELODY
4 : FULL STEREO TRACK

C VERSION

ALMOST LIKE BEING IN LOVE

FROM BRIGADOON

LYRICS BY ALAN JAY LERNER
MUSIC BY FREDERICK LOEWE

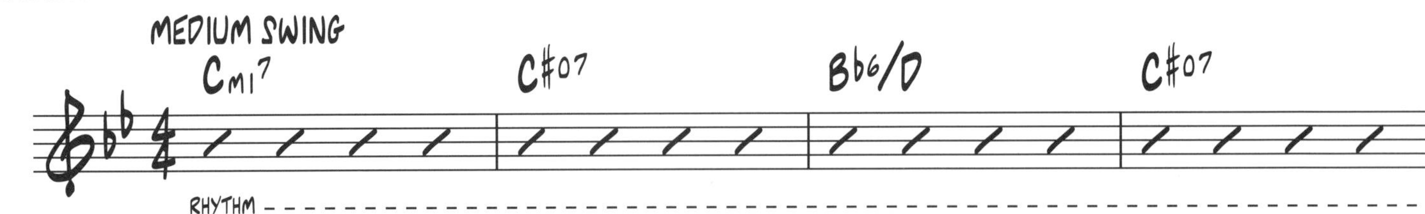

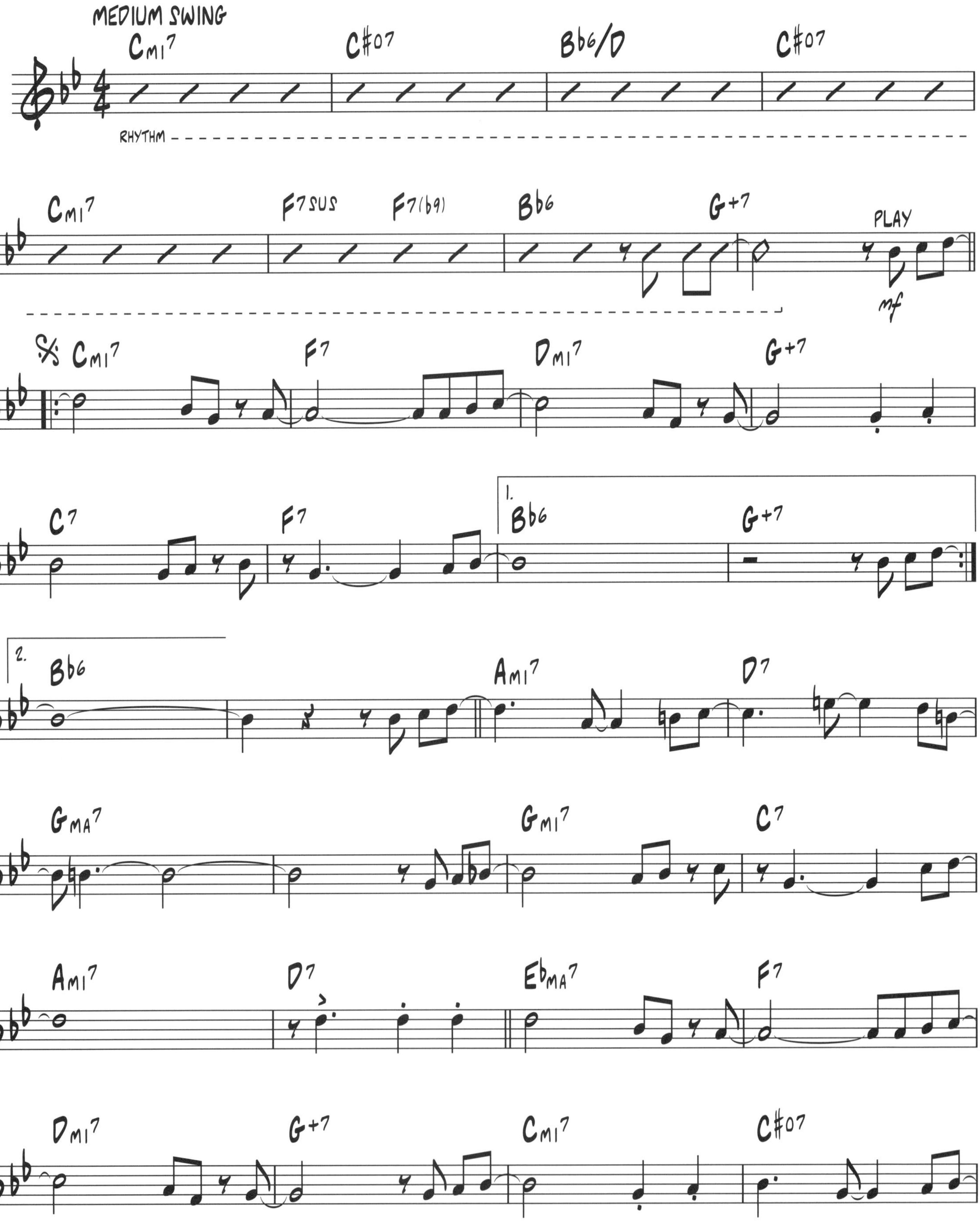

MEDIUM SWING
Cmi7
C#o7
Bb6/D
C#o7
RHYTHM
Cmi7
F7SUS
F7(b9)
Bb6
G+7
PLAY
mf
Cmi7
F7
Dmi7
G+7
C7
F7
1.
Bb6
G+7
2.
Bb6
Ami7
D7
Gma7
Gmi7
C7
Ami7
D7
Ebma7
F7
Dmi7
G+7
Cmi7
C#o7

TO CODA

Bb6/D C#07 Cmi7 F7SUS F7(b9) Bb6

SOLO BREAK SOLOS (2 CHORUSES)

Cmi7 F7 Dmi7 G+7

C7 F7 Bb6 G+7 Cmi7 F7

Dmi7 G+7 C7 F7 Bb6

Ami7 D7 Gma7 Gmi7 C7

Ami7 D7 Ebma7 F7 Dmi7 G+7

Cmi7 C#07 Bb6/D C#07 Cmi7 F7SUS F7(b9)

Bb6 G+7 D.S. AL CODA TAKE REPEAT

LAST X ONLY

CODA F7SUS F7(b9) E7(b5)

Eb7 D+7(#9) Db7(b5) Cmi7 Bma7 Bbma7

CD #1

5: SPLIT TRACK/MELODY

6: FULL STEREO TRACK

C VERSION

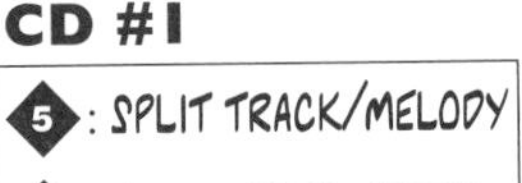

BLUE SKIES

FROM BETSY

WORDS AND MUSIC BY
IRVING BERLIN

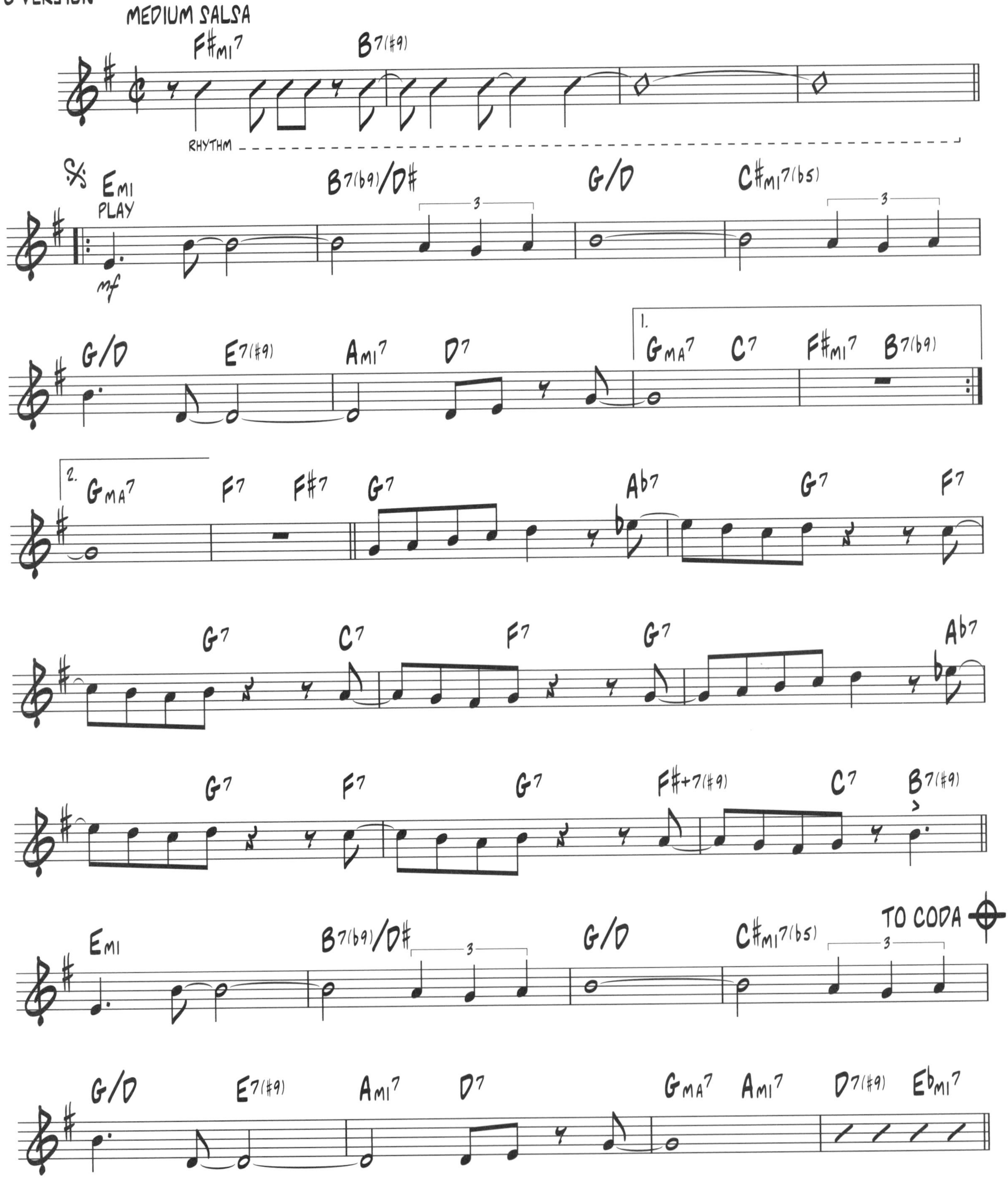
MEDIUM SALSA
F#MI7 B7(#9)
RHYTHM
EMI B7(b9)/D# G/D C#MI7(b5)
PLAY
mf
G/D E7(#9) AMI7 D7
1. GMA7 C7 F#MI7 B7(b9)
2. GMA7 F7 F#7 G7 Ab7 G7 F7
G7 C7 F7 G7 Ab7
G7 F7 G7 F#+7(#9) C7 B7(#9)
TO CODA
EMI B7(b9)/D# G/D C#MI7(b5)
G/D E7(#9) AMI7 D7 GMA7 AMI7 D7(#9) EbMI7

SOLOS (2 FULL CHORUSES)
EMI
B7(b9)/D#
G/D
C#MI7(b5)
G/D E7(#9)
AMI7 D7
1.
GMA7 C7
F#MI7 B7(b9)
2.
GMA7
F7 F#7
G7
Ab7 G7
F7 G7
C7 D7
G7
Ab7 G7
F7 G7
F#7 B7
EMI
B7(b9)/D#
G/D
C#MI7(b5)
G/D E7(#9)
AMI7 D7
GMA7 AMI7
D7(#9) EbMI7
D.S. AL CODA
TAKE REPEAT
CODA
G/D
E7(#9)
AMI7 D7
GMA7 E7(#9)
AMI7 D7(b9)
GMA7
E7(#9)
AMI7 D7
GMA7 Bb7
Eb7 Ab7
3
GMA7
E7(#9)
AMI7 D7
GMA7
F7
F#7
G6

CD #1

9 : SPLIT TRACK/MELODY
10 : FULL STEREO TRACK

COME RAIN OR COME SHINE

FROM ST. LOUIS WOMAN

WORDS BY JOHNNY MERCER
MUSIC BY HAROLD ARLEN

C VERSION

TO CODA
DMI7 B+7(#9) Bb7(b5) A7(b9) D7(#9) G7 G+7 C7SUS C7(b9)
SOLO
FMA7 EMI7 A+7 DMI7
G7SUS G+7 C7SUS C7(b9) FMA7 Db7 CMI7 B7(b5)
BbMI7 FMI6 B7(b5) BbMI7 Ab7 GMI7(b5) C7(b9)
BMI7(b5) E7(b9) AMI7(b5) D7(b9) AMI7(b5) D+7(b9) G7 C7SUS C7(b9)
FMA7 EMI7 A+7 DMI7 Eb7(b5) DMI7
AbMI7 Db7 F#MI7 B+7 EMI7 A+7 EMI7 Eb7(b5)
D7SUS EMI7 Fo7 D7/F# G7SUS AMI7 BbMA7 A+7 A7(b9)
D.S. AL CODA
DMI7 B+7(#9) Bb7(b5) A7(b9) D7(#9) G7 G+7 C7SUS C7(b9)
CODA
4X'S
D7(#9) G7 A+7 DMI7
1ST X ONLY
RIT. LAST TIME

CD #1

11 : SPLIT TRACK/MELODY

12 : FULL STEREO TRACK

DESAFINADO

C VERSION

ORIGINAL TEXT BY NEWTON MENDONÇA
MUSIC BY ANTONIO CARLOS JOBIM

D7(b9) G7SUS G+7 C7SUS C7(b9) FMA7
G7(b5) GMI7 C7 AMI7(b5)
D+7(#9) D7(b9) GMI7 Eb7 FMA7 Ab0
G7SUS G7 G7SUS G7 Eb7SUS Eb7 Eb7SUS Eb7 G7SUS G7
TO CODA
SOLO
GMI7 C7 FMA7 Gb7(b5) FMA7 G7(b5)
GMI7 C7 AMI7(b5) D7(b9) GMI7 EMI7(b5) A7(b9) 1. DMA7
D7(b9) G7 G7(b9) GbMA7 Gb7(b5) 2. DMI7 E7
AMA7 Ab+7 G7 Gb7 AMA7 Bb0 BMI7
E7 AMA7 F#MI7 BMI7 E7 CMA7
C#0 DMI7 G7 GMI7 D7(b9) GMI7 C7
D.S. AL CODA
CODA
FMA7 Gb7(b5) FMA7 Gb7(b5)
3
FMA7 Gb7(b5) FMA7

CD #1

13: SPLIT TRACK/MELODY

14: FULL STEREO TRACK

DON'T GET AROUND MUCH ANYMORE

FROM SOPHISTICATED LADY

C VERSION

WORDS AND MUSIC BY DUKE ELLINGTON
AND BOB RUSSELL

SOLO
CMA7
A7
D7
G7
1.
CMA7
DMI7
G7
2.
CMA7
Ab7
GMI7
C7
FMA7
F#07
CMA7/G
C7
FMA7
F#07
B7(b9)
EMI7
Eb07
DMI7
G7
CMA7
A7
D7
G7
CMA7
N.C./G
D.S. AL CODA
TAKE REPEAT
CODA
CMA7
G7
RHYTHM
CMA7
G7
RHYTHM
CMA7
Ab7
G7
C6
RHYTHM

CD #1

15: SPLIT TRACK/MELODY

16: FULL STEREO TRACK

C VERSION

FOR ALL WE KNOW

FROM THE MOTION PICTURE LOVERS AND OTHER STRANGERS

WORDS BY ROBB WILSON AND ARTHUR JAMES
MUSIC BY FRED KARLIN

MEDIUM BOSSA

BMA7 EMA7(b5) BMA7 EMA7(b5) PLAY

RHYTHM

mf

Eb6 F7 F+7 Bb7 Bb7SUS Bb7(b9)

EbMA7 AbMA7 GMI7 C+7(b9) FMI7 B7(b5) Bb7SUS Bb7(b9)

GMI7 Gbo FMI7 Bb7

CMI7 /G Gbo FMI7 Bb7SUS Bb7(b9)

𝄋 Eb6 F7 F+7 Bb7 Bb7SUS Bb7(b9)

EbMA7 AbMA7 GMI7 C+7(b9) FMI7 B7(b5) Bb7SUS Bb7(b9)

EbMA7 Ab7(b5) G7 Db7(b5) C7SUS C7(b9)

TO CODA
Fmi7 B7(b5) Bb7sus Bb7(b9) Bma7 Ema7(b5)
SOLO
Eb6 F7 F+7 Bb7 Bb7sus Bb7(b9) Ebma7 Abma7
Gmi7 C+7(b9) Fmi7 B7(b5) Bb7sus Bb7(b9) Gmi7 Gbo
Fmi7 Bb7 Cmi7 /G Gbo Fmi7
Bb7sus Bb7(b9) Eb6 F7 F+7 Bb7 Bb7sus Bb7(b9)
Ebma7 Abma7 Gmi7 C+7(b9) Fmi7 B7(b5) Bb7sus Bb7(b9)
Ebma7 Ab7(b5) G7 Db7(b5) C7sus C7(b9)
Fmi7 B7(b5) Bb7sus Bb7(b9) Bma7 Ema7(b5) D.S. AL CODA
CODA
Bma7 Ema7(b5) Bma7 Ema7(b5) Ebma7(b5)
RIT.
RHYTHM

CD #1

17: SPLIT TRACK/MELODY
18: FULL STEREO TRACK

I GOTTA RIGHT TO SING THE BLUES

WORDS BY TED KOEHLER
MUSIC BY HAROLD ARLEN

C VERSION

DMI7(b5) G+7 G7 C7
Ab7(b5) GMI7 C7
TO CODA
CMI7 Gb7 F7 Bb7 Eb7 Bb7 A7 Ab7 G7
SOLO
C7 F7
Bb7 DMI7(b5) G7
C7 F7
Bb7 Bb7SUS Bbo7 Bb7 EbMI6/Bb Bbo7 Bb7 A+7 Ab7 G7
D.S. AL CODA
CODA Bb7 B7(b5) Bb7(b5)
RIT.

CD #1

19 : SPLIT TRACK/MELODY
20 : FULL STEREO TRACK

I WISH I DIDN'T LOVE YOU SO

FROM THE PARAMOUNT PICTURE THE PERILS OF PAULINE

WORDS AND MUSIC BY
FRANK LOESSER

C VERSION

SOLO
Eb6 AbMA7 GMI7 C7 FMI7 Bb7(b9) EbMA7 BbMI7 Eb7 AbMA7 Db7
GMI7 C7 FMI7 Bb7SUS G+7 Gb7 FMI7 E7(b5)
Eb6 AbMA7 GMI7 C7 FMI7 Bb7(b9) EbMA7 A+7(b9) AbMA7 Db7
GMI7 C7 FMI7 Bb7SUS Eb6 AbMA7 Eb6
GMI7(b5) C7(b9) GMI7(b5) C7(b9) FMI7
G+7(b9) Db7(b5) C7 C7(b5) F7SUS F7 FMI7 E7(b5)
Eb6 AbMA7 GMI7 C7 FMI7 Bb7(b9) EbMA7 A+7(b9) AbMA7 Db7
GMI7 C7 FMI7 Bb7SUS Eb6 AbMA7 Eb6
D.S. AL CODA
CODA
AbMA7 Db7 Gb7 Cb7 FMI7 E7(b5) EbMA7

CD #2

1 : SPLIT TRACK/MELODY
2 : FULL STEREO TRACK

I'LL TAKE ROMANCE

LYRICS BY OSCAR HAMMERSTEIN II
MUSIC BY BEN OAKLAND

C VERSION

MEDIUM SWING

F6 Ab7 Db6 C7SUS F6 Ab7 Db6 C7SUS

RHYTHM

2 FEEL
F6 Dmi7 Gmi7 C7 /Bb Ami7 Ab7 Db6 Gbma7
PLAY
mf

A+7(b9) D7(b9) Gmi7 C7(b9) F6 Ab7 Db6 C7SUS

F6 Dmi7 Gmi7 C7 /Bb Ami7 Ab7 Db6 Gbma7

4 FEEL
A+7(b9) D7(b9) Gmi7 C7(b9) F6 C7SUS F6

Ebmi7 Ab7 Dbma7 Bbmi7 Ebmi7 Ab7 Dbma7

C#mi7 F#7 Bma7 Ema7 A+7 Ab7 Gmi7 C7 C#o

2 FEEL
Dmi7 /C Bmi7(b5) Bbmi6 Ami7 Ab7 Db6 Gbma7
TO CODA

A+7(b9) D7(b9) Gmi7 C7(b9) F6
SOLO BREAK
SOLOS (2 CHORUSES)
4 FEEL
F6 Dmi7 Gmi7 C7 /Bb Ami7 Ab7 Db6 Gbma7 A+7(b9) D7(b9)
Gmi7 C7(b9) F6 Ab7 Db6 C7 F6 Dmi7 Gmi7 C7 /Bb
Ami7 Ab7 Db6 Gbma7 A+7(b9) D7(b9) Gmi7 C7(b9) F6 C7sus F6
Ebmi7 Ab7 Dbma7 Bbmi7 Ebmi7 Ab7 Dbma7 C#mi7 F#7 Bma7 Ema7
A+7 Ab7 Dbma7 C7 C#o Dmi7 /C Bmi7(b5) Bbmi6 Ami7 Ab7
D.S. AL CODA
Db6 Gbma7 A+7(b9) D7(b9) Gmi7 C7(b9) F6 Ab7 Db6 C7
CODA
A+7(b9) D7(b9) Gmi7 C7(b9) F6 Ab7 Db6 C7sus
F6 Ab7 Db6 C7sus Gbma7 Fma7

CD #2

3 : SPLIT TRACK/MELODY
4 : FULL STEREO TRACK

C VERSION

IN THE WEE SMALL HOURS OF THE MORNING

WORDS BY BOB HILLIARD
MUSIC BY DAVID MANN

C6
Db7(b5)
SOLO
CMA7
C7
C6
C+
CMA7
C+
DMI7
G7
DMI7
G7
/F
EMI7(b5)
A7
/G
F#MI7
B7
EMI7
Eb7(b5)
DMI7
G7SUS
CMA7
Bb7(b5)
CMA7
Bb7(b5)
CMA7
Bb7(b5)
A7
A+7
A7
DMI7
D#07
EMI7
Bb7
A+7
DMI7
G7
/F
EMI7
A+7
DMI7
G7(b9)
FMA7
Eb6
DMI7
DbMA7
CMA7
RIT.

CD #2
5 : SPLIT TRACK/MELODY
6 : FULL STEREO TRACK
JUST IN TIME
FROM BELLS ARE RINGING
WORDS BY BETTY COMDEN AND ADOLPH GREEN
MUSIC BY JULE STYNE
C VERSION
MEDIUM SWING
F7 Ab7 A7 Bb7 Db7(b5) Cmi7 F7(b9)
RHYTHM
BbMA7 Ami7 D7(#9)
PLAY
mf
G7SUS G7(b9) C7 Bb6/D Eb° C7/E
F7SUS F7(b9) Bb7
EbMA7 A+7(b9) AbMA7 Ami7 D7(b9)
Gmi Gmi/F# Gmi/F Emi7(b5) A+7(b9)
Bb6 A7(b9) Ab7 G7
C7 F7SUS F7 Bb6 Eb7 Dmi7 Db7(b5)

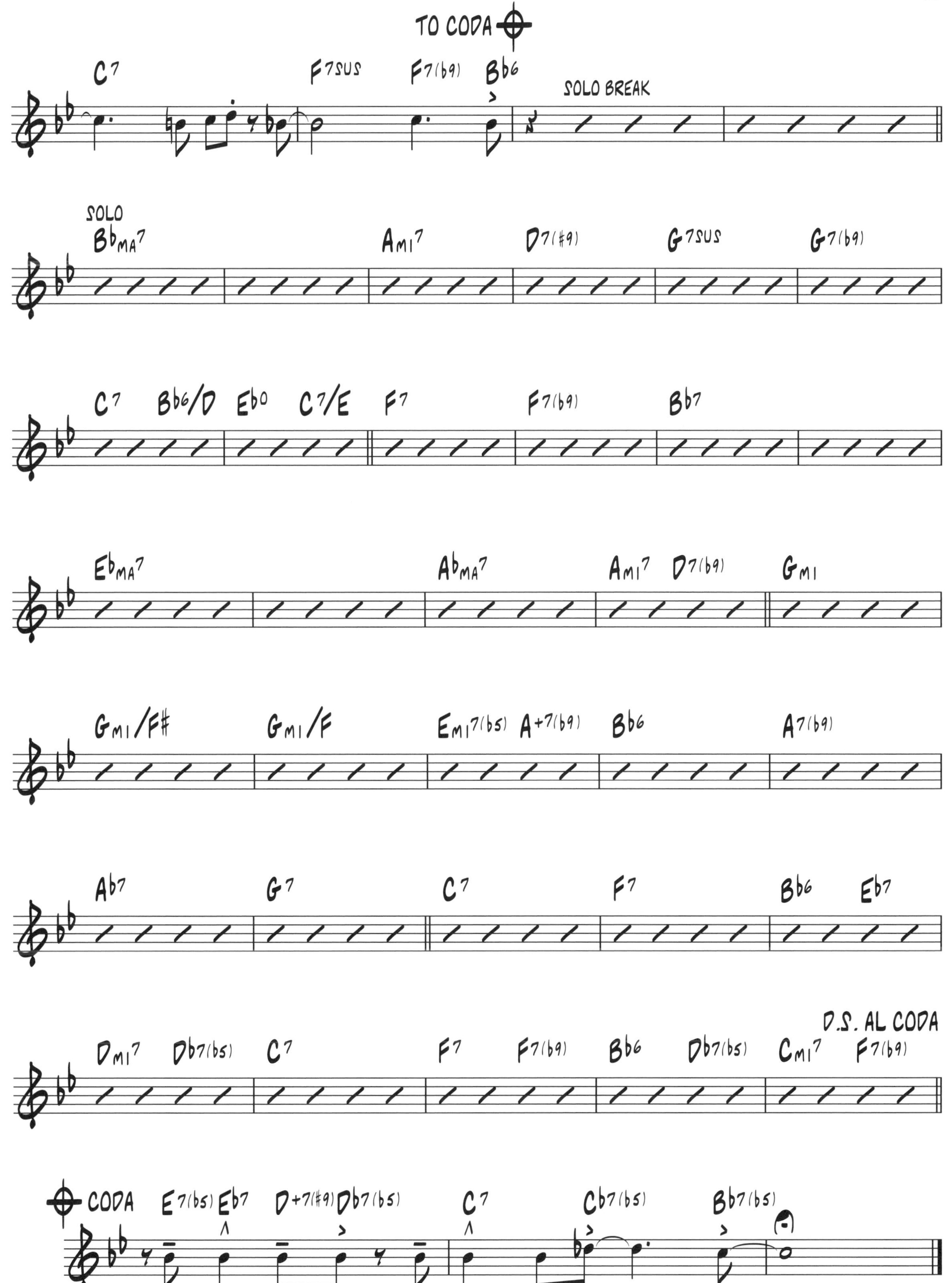
TO CODA
C7
F7SUS
F7(b9)
Bb6
SOLO BREAK
SOLO
BbMA7
AMI7
D7(#9)
G7SUS
G7(b9)
C7
Bb6/D
Ebo
C7/E
F7
F7(b9)
Bb7
EbMA7
AbMA7
AMI7
D7(b9)
GMI
GMI/F#
GMI/F
EMI7(b5)
A+7(b9)
Bb6
A7(b9)
Ab7
G7
C7
F7
Bb6
Eb7
D.S. AL CODA
DMI7
Db7(b5)
C7
F7
F7(b9)
Bb6
Db7(b5)
CMI7
F7(b9)
CODA
E7(b5)
Eb7
D+7(#9)
Db7(b5)
C7
Cb7(b5)
Bb7(b5)

CD #2

7 : SPLIT TRACK/MELODY
8 : FULL STEREO TRACK

LIKE SOMEONE IN LOVE

WORDS BY JOHNNY BURKE
MUSIC BY JIMMY VAN HEUSEN

C VERSION

MEDIUM BOSSA

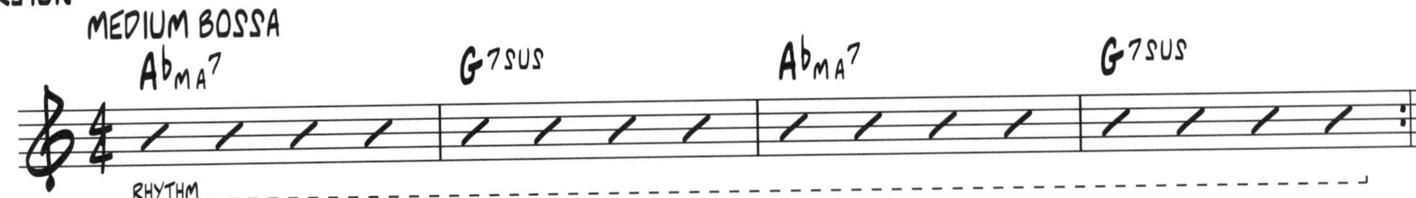

TO CODA
EMI7 A7 DMI7 G7(b9) C6 AbMA7 G7SUS
SOLO
CMA7 /B AMI7 /G D7/F# F7(b5) EMI7 Eb7 DMI7
F#MI7 B7 CMA7 GMI7/C C7 F6 BMI7 E7
AMA7 Bb7(b5) AMI7 D7 DMI7 G7 AbMI7 Db7
CMA7 /B AMI7 /G D7/F# F7(b5) EMI7 Eb7 DMI7 F#MI7 B7
CMA7 GMI7 C7 F6 BMI7 E7 AMA7
D.S. AL CODA
D7 D#o7 EMI7 A7 DMI7 G7(b9) C6 AbMA7 G7SUS
CODA
C6 AbMA7 G7SUS C6 AbMA7 G7SUS
C6 AbMA7 G7SUS CMA7

CD #2

LOLLIPOPS AND ROSES

WORDS AND MUSIC BY
TONY VELONA

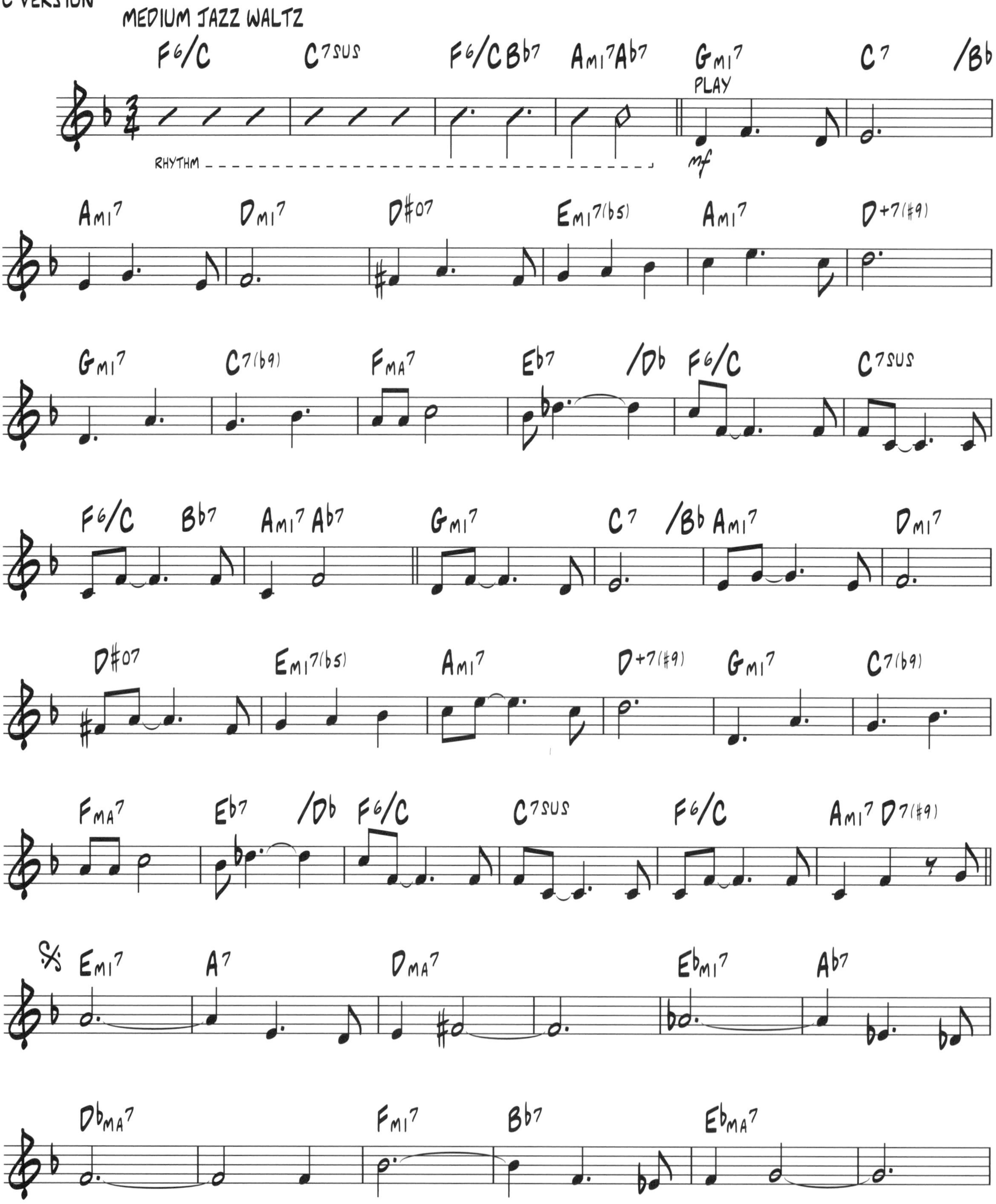

C VERSION

MEDIUM JAZZ WALTZ

DMI7 G7(b9) GMI7 C7SUS Ab7 GMI7
C7 /Bb AMI7 DMI7 D#07 EMI7(b5)
AMI7 D+7(#9) GMI7 C7(b9) FMA7
TO CODA
Eb7 /Db F6/C C7SUS F6/C A+7 Ab7
SOLO
GMI7 C7 /Bb AMI7 DMI7 D#07 EMI7(b5)
AMI7 D+7(#9) GMI7 C7(b9) FMA7 Eb7 /Db
1. 2. D.S. AL CODA
F6/C C7SUS F6/C AMI7 Ab7 AMI7 D7(#9)
CODA
F6/C C7SUS F6/C D7(#9)
GMI7 C7SUS GMI7 GbMA7 FMA7

CD #2

11: SPLIT TRACK/MELODY
12: FULL STEREO TRACK

LOVE IS JUST AROUND THE CORNER

FROM THE PARAMOUNT PICTURE HERE IS MY HEART

WORDS AND MUSIC BY LEO ROBIN
AND LEWIS E. GENSLER

C VERSION

SOLOS (2 CHORUSES)
G7/B C7/Bb F6/A D+7(b9) G7/B C7/Bb F6/A D+7(b9)
G7/B C7/Bb F6/A Ab7 G7 C7(b9) F6 Ab7/C
G7/B C7/Bb F6/A D+7(b9) G7/B C7/Bb F6/A D+7(b9)
G7/B C7/Bb F6/A Ab7 G7 C7(b9) F6 Emi7 A+7(b9)
Dmi7 B7(#9) Emi7 A+7(b9) Dmi7 G7 Emi7 A7
Dmi7 G7 Gmi7 C7(b9) G7/B C7/Bb F6/A D+7(b9) G7/B C7/Bb
F6/A D+7(b9) G7/B C7/Bb F6/A Ab7 G7 C7(b9) F6 D.S. AL CODA
CODA
G7 C7SUS C7(b9) F6 Ab7 G7 C7SUS C7(b9) F6 D+7(#9)
G7 C7SUS C7(b9) F6 Bb7 A7 Ab7 G7(b5) Gb7(b5) FMA7(b5)

CD #2

13: SPLIT TRACK/MELODY

14: FULL STEREO TRACK

C VERSION

MY IDEAL

FROM THE PARAMOUNT PICTURE PLAYBOY OF PARIS

WORDS BY LEO ROBIN
MUSIC BY RICHARD A. WHITING AND NEWELL CHASE

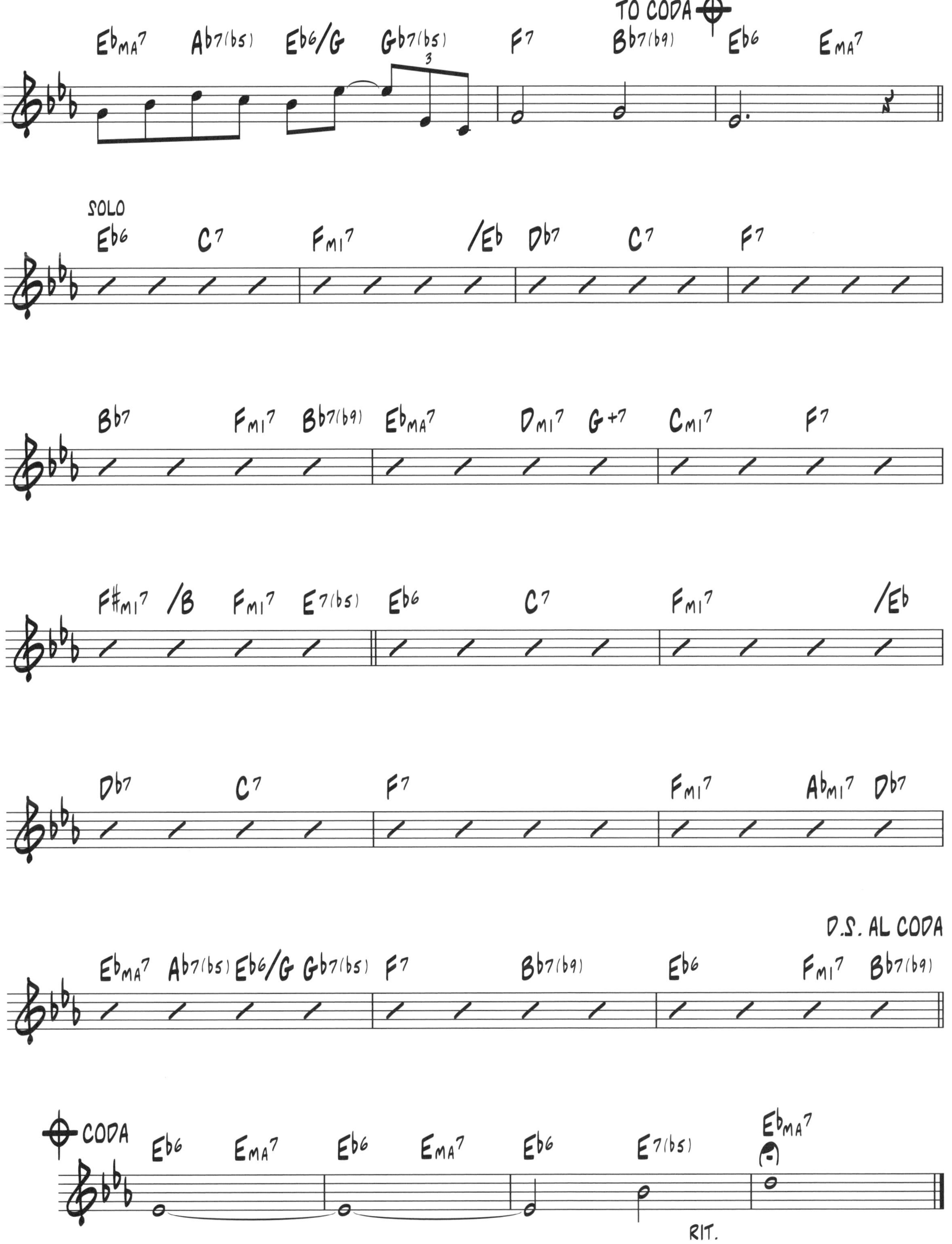
TO CODA
Ebma7 Ab7(b5) Eb6/G Gb7(b5) F7 Bb7(b9) Eb6 Ema7
SOLO
Eb6 C7 Fmi7 /Eb Db7 C7 F7
Bb7 Fmi7 Bb7(b9) Ebma7 Dmi7 G+7 Cmi7 F7
F#mi7 /B Fmi7 E7(b5) Eb6 C7 Fmi7 /Eb
Db7 C7 F7 Fmi7 Abmi7 Db7
D.S. AL CODA
Ebma7 Ab7(b5) Eb6/G Gb7(b5) F7 Bb7(b9) Eb6 Fmi7 Bb7(b9)
CODA
Eb6 Ema7 Eb6 Ema7 Eb6 E7(b5) Ebma7
RIT.

CD #2

15: SPLIT TRACK/MELODY
16: FULL STEREO TRACK

C VERSION

ON A SLOW BOAT TO CHINA

BY FRANK LOESSER

SOLO
Bb6 B07 Cmi7 C#07
Bb6/D D7sus D7(b9) Ebma7 Dmi7(b5) G+7(b9)
1.
Cmi7 Emi7 A7(b9) Bbma7 Ab7(b5) G7
C7sus C7 Cmi7 F7
2.
Cmi7 /Bb Ab7 Bbma7 Ab7 G7
D.S. AL CODA
TAKE 2ND ENDING
C7sus C7 Cmi7 F7 Bb6 Db7 C7 B7
CODA
Bb6 Db7 C7 B7 Bb6 Db7 C7 B7
Bb6 Db7 C7 B7(b5) F+7 Bb6

CD #2

17 : SPLIT TRACK/MELODY
18 : FULL STEREO TRACK

TOO LATE NOW

FROM ROYAL WEDDING

WORDS BY ALAN JAY LERNER
MUSIC BY BURTON LANE

CMA7 /B AMI7 DMI7 G7SUS CMA7 /B AMI7
DMI7 G7SUS CMA7 /B AMI7 /G F#MI7(b5) F7(b5)
TO CODA
EMI7 Eb7 DMI7 G7 C6 DbMA7
SOLO
CMA7 AMI7 DMI7 G7SUS CMA7 AMI7
DMI7 G7SUS CMA7 AMI7
1.
F#MI7(b5) B+7 EMI7 Eb7 DMI7 G7
2.
F#MI7(b5) F7(b5) EMI7 Eb7 DMI7 G7 C6 BMI7 E+7
AMI6 BMI7 E7 AMI7 D+7 GMI6
AMI7 D7(b9) DMI7 G7 CMA7 AMI7 DMI7 G7SUS CMA7 AMI7
DMI7 G7SUS CMA7 AMI7 F#MI7(b5) F7(b5) EMI7 Eb7 DMI7 G7 C6
D.S. AL CODA
CODA
EMI7 Eb7 DMI7 G7 Ab6 Bb6 C6
RIT.

CD #2

19 : SPLIT TRACK/MELODY

20 : FULL STEREO TRACK

YOU ARE TOO BEAUTIFUL

FROM HALLELUJAH, I'M A BUM

WORDS BY LORENZ HART
MUSIC BY RICHARD RODGERS

C VERSION

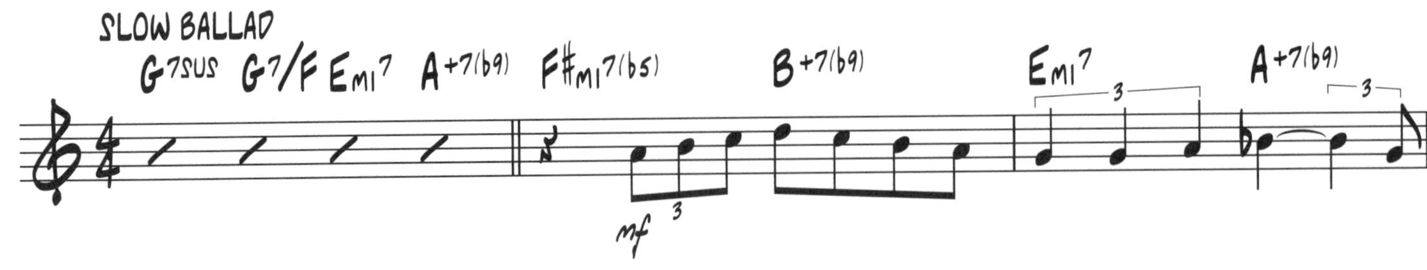

BMI7(b5) E7(b9) AMI7 D7SUS D7 Ab7(b5) G7 G7(b9)
F#MI7(b5) B+7(b9) EMI7 A+7(b9) DMI7 G+7(b9)
CMA7 GMI7 C7(b9) FMA7 Bb7 AMI7 D7SUS D7
TO CODA
D7 D+7 G7SUS G7(b9) C6 EMI7 A+7(b9)
SOLO
F#MI7(b5) B+7(b9) EMI7 A+7(b9)
DMI7 G+7(b9) CMA7 GMI7 C7(b9) FMA7 Bb7 AMI7 D7SUS D7
1.
DMI7 G7(b9) EMI7 A+7(b9)
2.
D7 D+7 G7SUS G7(b9) C6 GMI7 C7
D.S. AL CODA
CODA
AbMA7 DbMA7 CMA7
RIT.

CD #1
7 : SPLIT TRACK/MELODY
8 : FULL STEREO TRACK
CAN'T HELP LOVIN' DAT MAN
FROM SHOW BOAT
LYRICS BY OSCAR HAMMERSTEIN II
MUSIC BY JEROME KERN
C VERSION
SLOW BLUES
RHYTHM
PLAY
mf
TO CODA
SOLO
D.S. AL CODA
CODA

CD #1
7 : SPLIT TRACK/MELODY
8 : FULL STEREO TRACK
CAN'T HELP LOVIN' DAT MAN
FROM SHOW BOAT
LYRICS BY OSCAR HAMMERSTEIN II
MUSIC BY JEROME KERN
Bb VERSION
SLOW BLUES
RHYTHM
PLAY
mf
TO CODA
SOLO
D.S. AL CODA
CODA

1: SPLIT TRACK/MELODY
2: FULL STEREO TRACK

ALL THE THINGS YOU ARE

FROM VERY WARM FOR MAY

LYRICS BY OSCAR HAMMERSTEIN II
MUSIC BY JEROME KERN

Bb VERSION

MEDIUM SWING

RHYTHM

Eb7(#9) D7(#9) 1. 2.

BASS

Gmi7 PLAY *mf* Cmi7 F7 Bbma7

Ebma7 Emi7 A7 Dma7

Dmi7 Gmi7 C7 Fma7

Bbma7 Bmi7(b5) E7 Ama7

Bmi7 E7 Ama7

G#mi7(b5) C#7 F#ma7 D+7(b9)

Gmi7 Cmi7 F7 Bbma7

EbMA7 Ab7 DMI7 C#o7
CMI7 F7 TO CODA Bb6 AMI7(b5) D7(b9)
SOLOS (2 CHORUSES)
GMI7 CMI7 F7 BbMA7 EbMA7
EMI7 A7 DMA7 DMI7 GMI7
C7 FMA7 BbMA7 BMI7(b5) E7 AMA7
BMI7 E7 AMA7
G#MI7(b5) C#7 F#MA7 D+7(b9) GMI7
CMI7 F7 BbMA7 EbMA7 Ab7
D.S. AL CODA
DMI7 C#o7 CMI7 F7 Bb6 AMI7(b5) D7(b9)
CODA N.C. Eb7(#9)
1ST X ONLY
1. D7(#9)
2. D7(#9)

CD #1

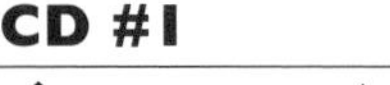

3: SPLIT TRACK/MELODY
4: FULL STEREO TRACK

ALMOST LIKE BEING IN LOVE

FROM BRIGADOON

LYRICS BY ALAN JAY LERNER
MUSIC BY FREDERICK LOEWE

Bb VERSION

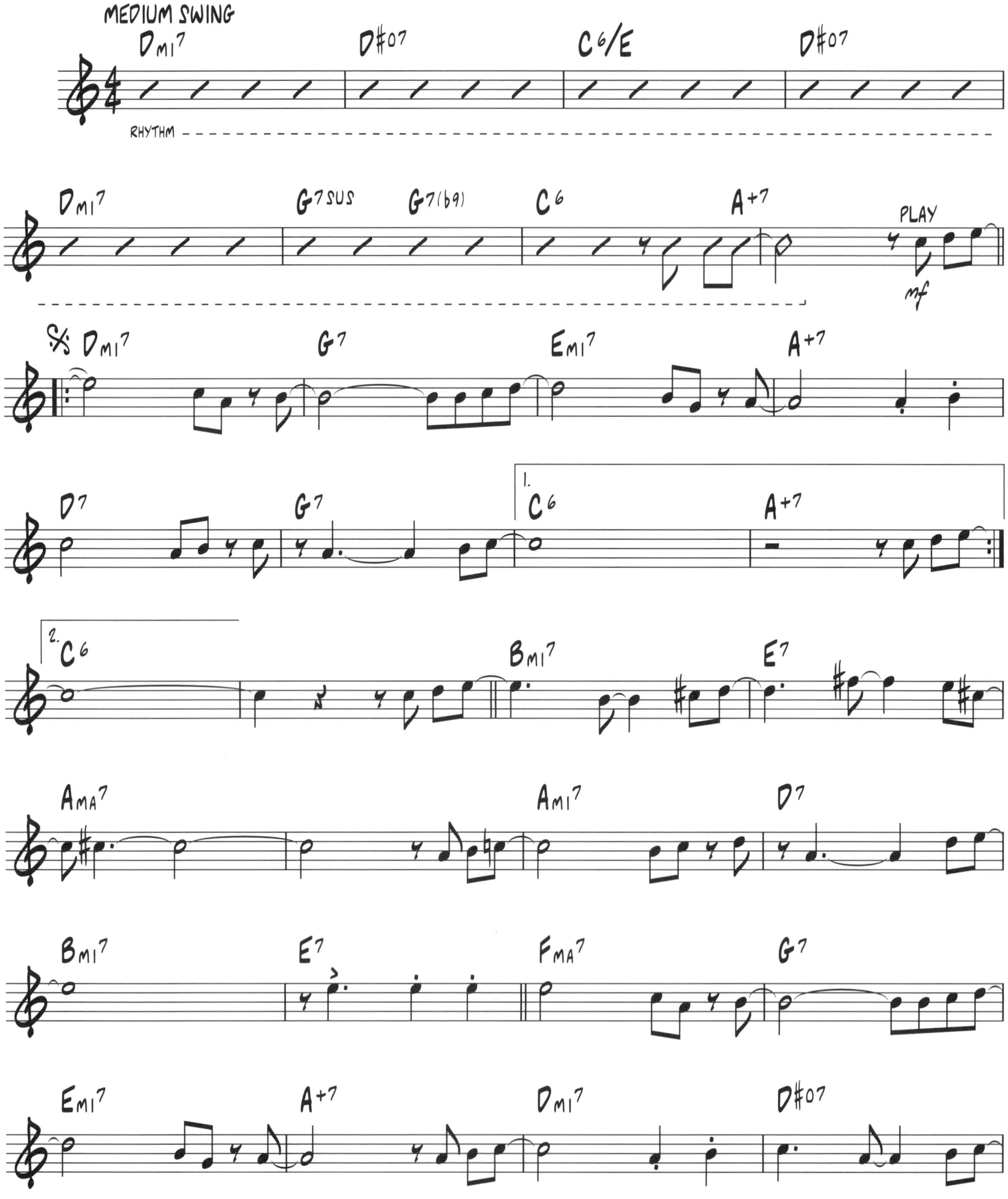

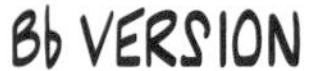

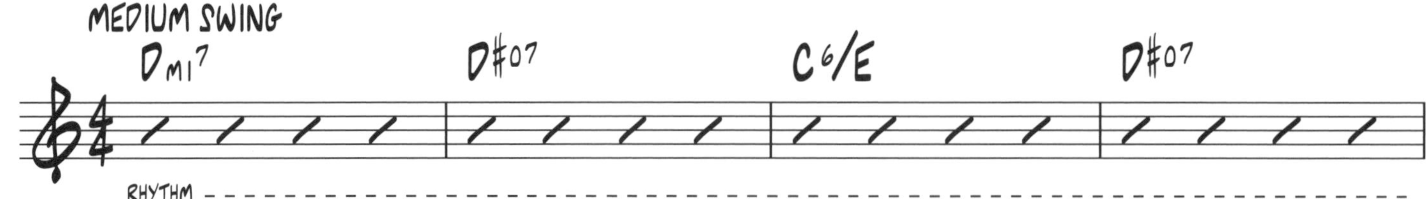

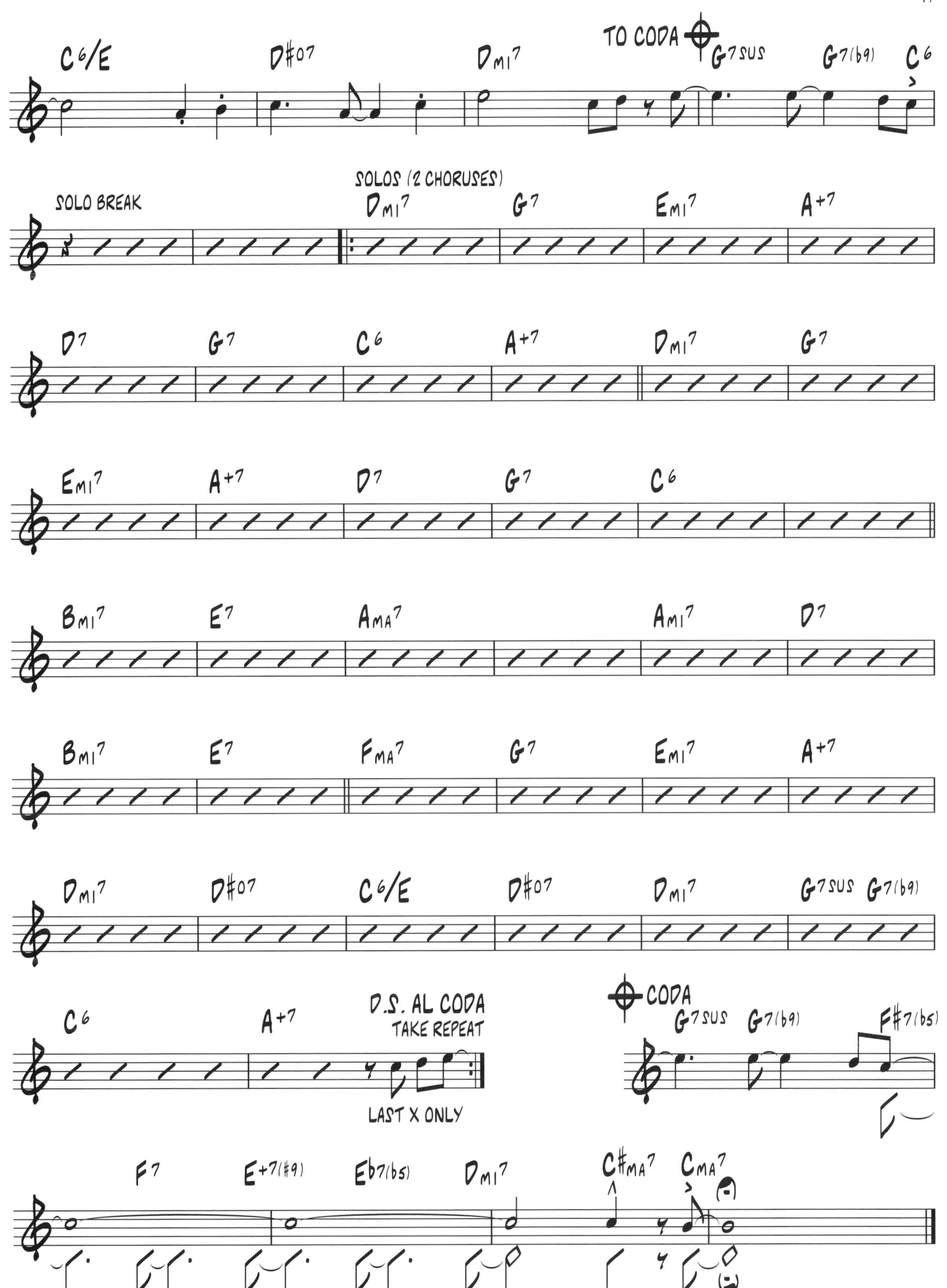

C6/E
D#o7
Dmi7
TO CODA
G7sus
G7(b9)
C6
SOLO BREAK
SOLOS (2 CHORUSES)
Dmi7
G7
Emi7
A+7
D7
G7
C6
A+7
Dmi7
G7
Emi7
A+7
D7
G7
C6
Bmi7
E7
Ama7
Ami7
D7
Bmi7
E7
Fma7
G7
Emi7
A+7
Dmi7
D#o7
C6/E
D#o7
Dmi7
G7sus
G7(b9)
C6
A+7
D.S. AL CODA
TAKE REPEAT
LAST X ONLY
CODA
G7sus
G7(b9)
F#7(b5)
F7
E+7(#9)
Eb7(b5)
Dmi7
C#ma7
Cma7

CD #1

5: SPLIT TRACK/MELODY
6: FULL STEREO TRACK

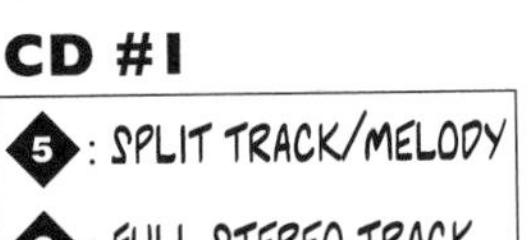

BLUE SKIES

FROM BETSY

WORDS AND MUSIC BY
IRVING BERLIN

B♭ VERSION

MEDIUM SALSA

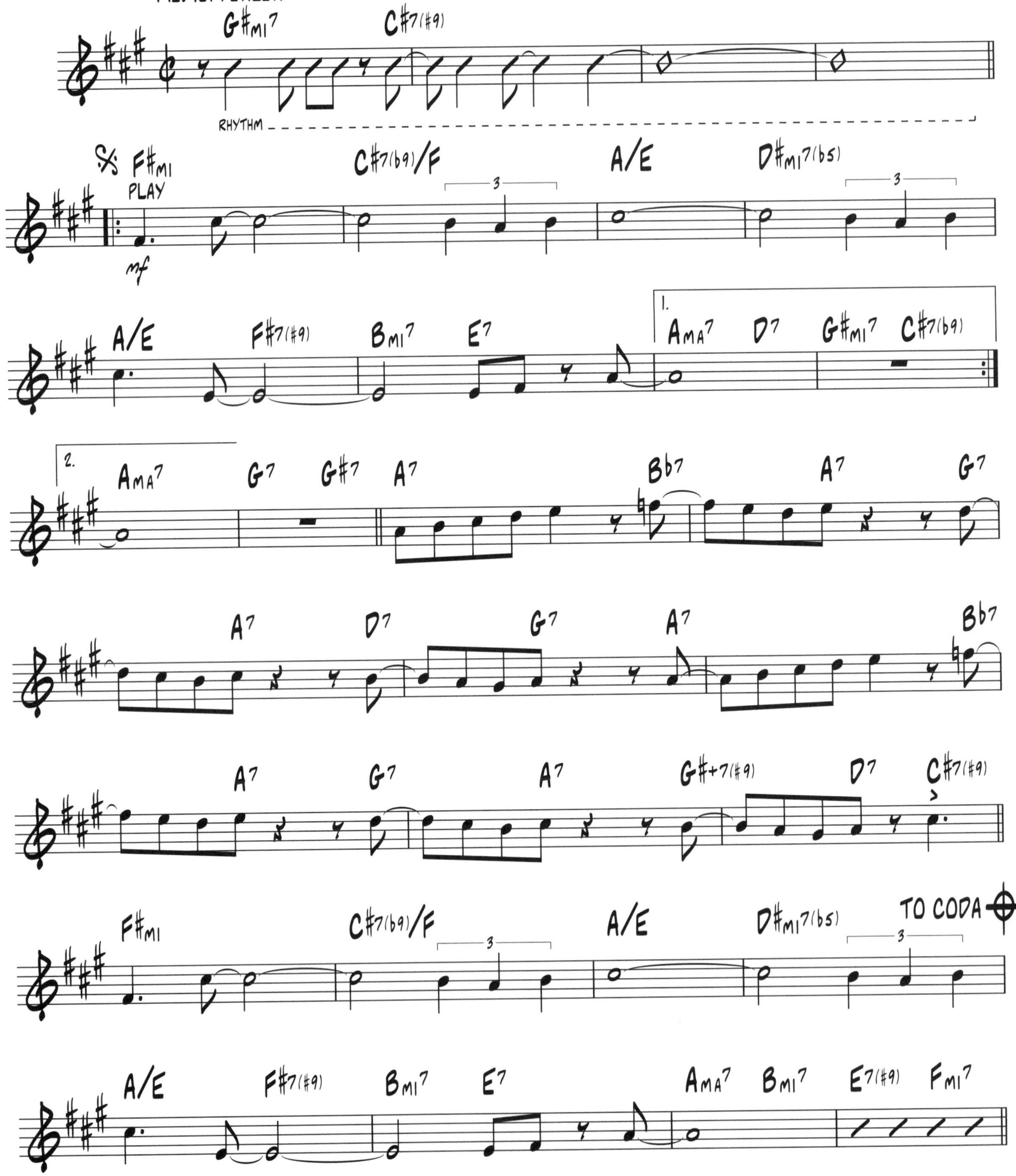

SOLOS (2 FULL CHORUSES)
F#MI C#7(b9)/F A/E D#MI7(b5) A/E F#7(#9)
BMI7 E7 1. AMA7 D7 G#MI7 C#7(b9) 2. AMA7 G7 G#7
A7 Bb7 A7 G7 A7 D7 E7
A7 Bb7 A7 G7 A7 G#7 C#7
F#MI C#7(b9)/F A/E D#MI7(b5)
D.S. AL CODA
TAKE REPEAT
A/E F#7(#9) BMI7 E7 AMA7 BMI7 E7(#9) FMI7
CODA
A/E F#7(#9) BMI7 E7 AMA7 F#7(#9) BMI7 E7(b9)
AMA7 F#7(#9) BMI7 E7 AMA7 C7 F7 Bb7
3
AMA7 F#7(#9) BMI7 E7 AMA7 G7 G#7 A6

CD #1
9: SPLIT TRACK/MELODY
10: FULL STEREO TRACK
COME RAIN OR COME SHINE
FROM ST. LOUIS WOMAN
WORDS BY JOHNNY MERCER
MUSIC BY HAROLD ARLEN
Bb VERSION
MEDIUM LATIN
RHYTHM
PLAY
mf

TO CODA
EMI7 C#+7(#9) C7(b5) B7(b9) E7(#9) A7 A+7 D7SUS D7(b9)
SOLO
GMA7 F#MI7 B+7 EMI7
A7SUS A+7 D7SUS D7(b9) GMA7 Eb7 DMI7 C#7(b5)
CMI7 GMI6 C#7(b5) CMI7 Bb7 AMI7(b5) D7(b9)
C#MI7(b5) F#7(b9) BMI7(b5) E7(b9) BMI7(b5) E+7(b9) A7 D7SUS D7(b9)
GMA7 F#MI7 B+7 EMI7 F7(b5) EMI7
BbMI7 Eb7 G#MI7 C#+7 F#MI7 B+7 F#MI7 F7(b5)
E7SUS F#MI7 G°7 E7/G# A7SUS BMI7 CMA7 B+7 B7(b9)
D.S. AL CODA
EMI7 C#+7(#9) C7(b5) B7(b9) E7(#9) A7 A+7 D7SUS D7(b9)
CODA
4X'S
E7(#9) A7 B+7 EMI7
1ST X ONLY
RIT. LAST TIME

CD #1

11 : SPLIT TRACK/MELODY
12 : FULL STEREO TRACK

DESAFINADO

ORIGINAL TEXT BY NEWTON MENDONÇA
MUSIC BY ANTONIO CARLOS JOBIM

B♭ VERSION

E7(b9) A7SUS A+7 D7SUS D7(b9) GMA7
A7(b5) AMI7 D7 BMI7(b5)
E+7(#9) E7(b9) AMI7 F7 GMA7 Bbo
A7SUS A7 A7SUS A7 F7SUS F7 F7SUS F7 A7SUS A7
TO CODA
SOLO
AMI7 D7 GMA7 Ab7(b5) GMA7 A7(b5)
AMI7 D7 BMI7(b5) E7(b9) AMI7 F#MI7(b5) B7(b9) EMA7
E7(b9) A7 A7(b9) AbMA7 Ab7(b5) EMI7 F#7
BMA7 Bb+7 A7 Ab7 BMA7 C0 C#MI7
F#7 BMA7 G#MI7 C#MI7 F#7 DMA7
D.S. AL CODA
D#0 EMI7 A7 AMI7 E7(b9) AMI7 D7
CODA
GMA7 Ab7(b5) GMA7 Ab7(b5)
GMA7 Ab7(b5) GMA7

CD #1

13: SPLIT TRACK/MELODY
14: FULL STEREO TRACK

DON'T GET AROUND MUCH ANYMORE

FROM SOPHISTICATED LADY

B♭ VERSION

WORDS AND MUSIC BY DUKE ELLINGTON
AND BOB RUSSELL

SOLO
DMA7
B7
E7
A7
1.
DMA7
EMI7
A7
2.
DMA7
Bb7
AMI7
D7
GMA7
G#o7
DMA7/A
D7
GMA7
G#o7
C#7(b9)
F#MI7
Fo7
EMI7
A7
DMA7
B7
E7
A7
DMA7
N.C./A
D.S. AL CODA
TAKE REPEAT
CODA
DMA7
A7
RHYTHM
DMA7
A7
RHYTHM
DMA7
Bb7
A7
D6
RHYTHM

15 : SPLIT TRACK/MELODY
16 : FULL STEREO TRACK

FOR ALL WE KNOW

FROM THE MOTION PICTURE LOVERS AND OTHER STRANGERS

WORDS BY ROBB WILSON AND ARTHUR JAMES
MUSIC BY FRED KARLIN

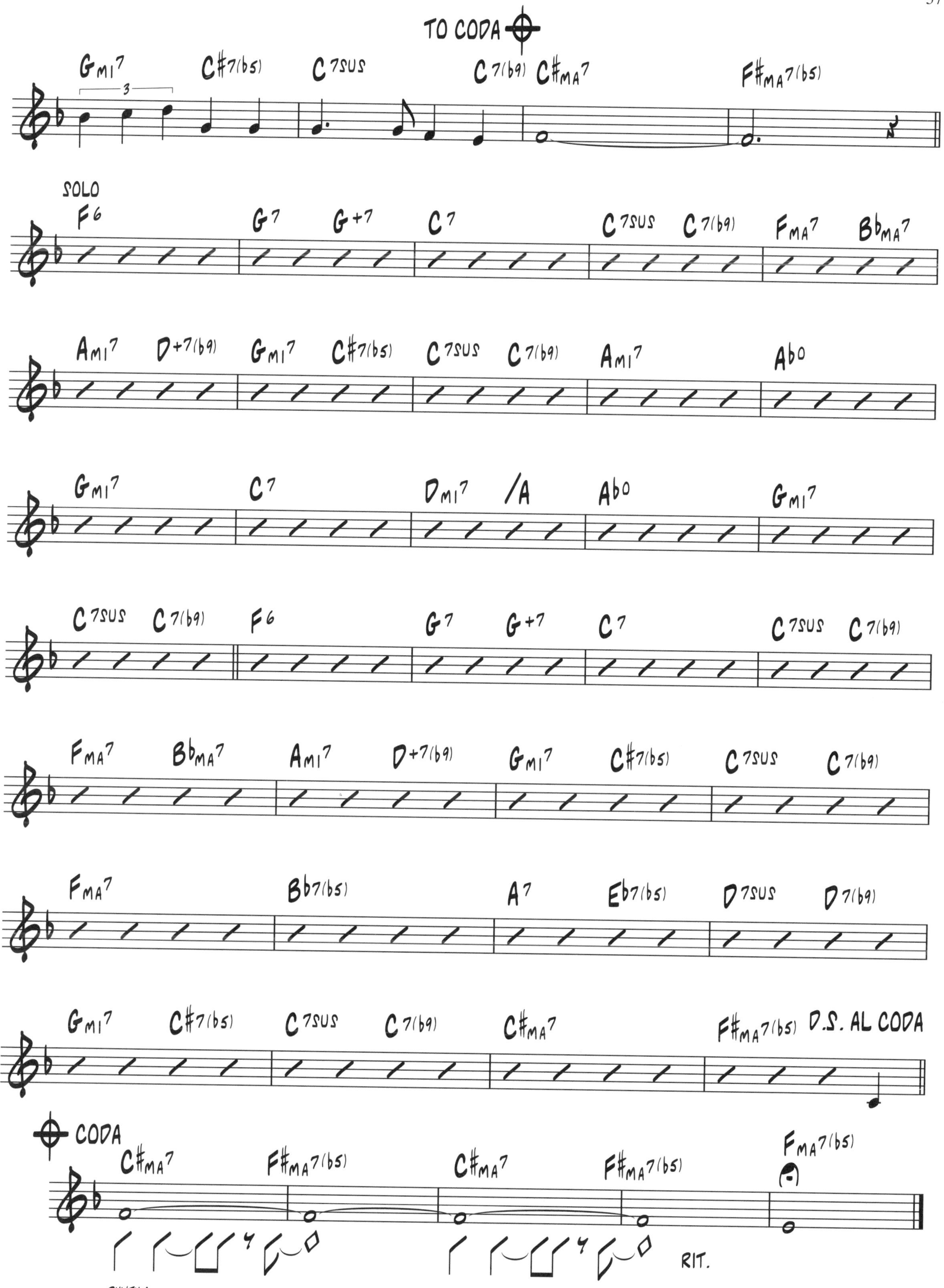
TO CODA
Gmi7 C#7(b5) C7sus C7(b9) C#ma7 F#ma7(b5)
SOLO
F6 G7 G+7 C7 C7sus C7(b9) Fma7 Bbma7
Ami7 D+7(b9) Gmi7 C#7(b5) C7sus C7(b9) Ami7 Abo
Gmi7 C7 Dmi7 /A Abo Gmi7
C7sus C7(b9) F6 G7 G+7 C7 C7sus C7(b9)
Fma7 Bbma7 Ami7 D+7(b9) Gmi7 C#7(b5) C7sus C7(b9)
Fma7 Bb7(b5) A7 Eb7(b5) D7sus D7(b9)
Gmi7 C#7(b5) C7sus C7(b9) C#ma7 F#ma7(b5) D.S. AL CODA
CODA
C#ma7 F#ma7(b5) C#ma7 F#ma7(b5) Fma7(b5)
RIT.
RHYTHM

CD #1

17 : SPLIT TRACK/MELODY
18 : FULL STEREO TRACK

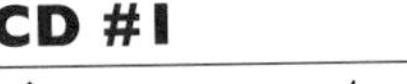

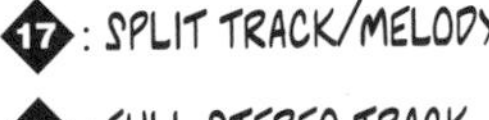

I GOTTA RIGHT TO SING THE BLUES

WORDS BY TED KOEHLER
MUSIC BY HAROLD ARLEN

Bb VERSION

SLOW BLUES

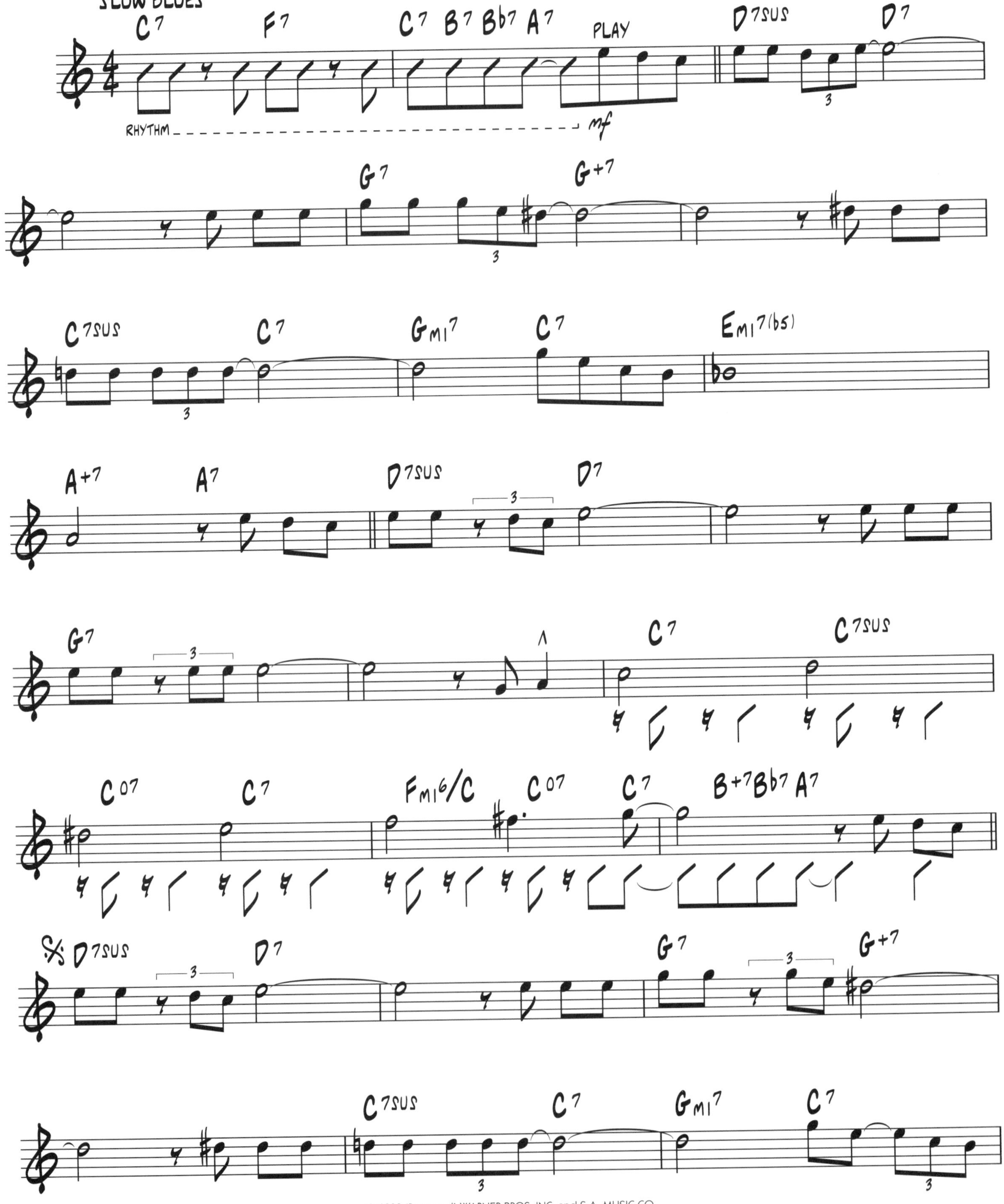

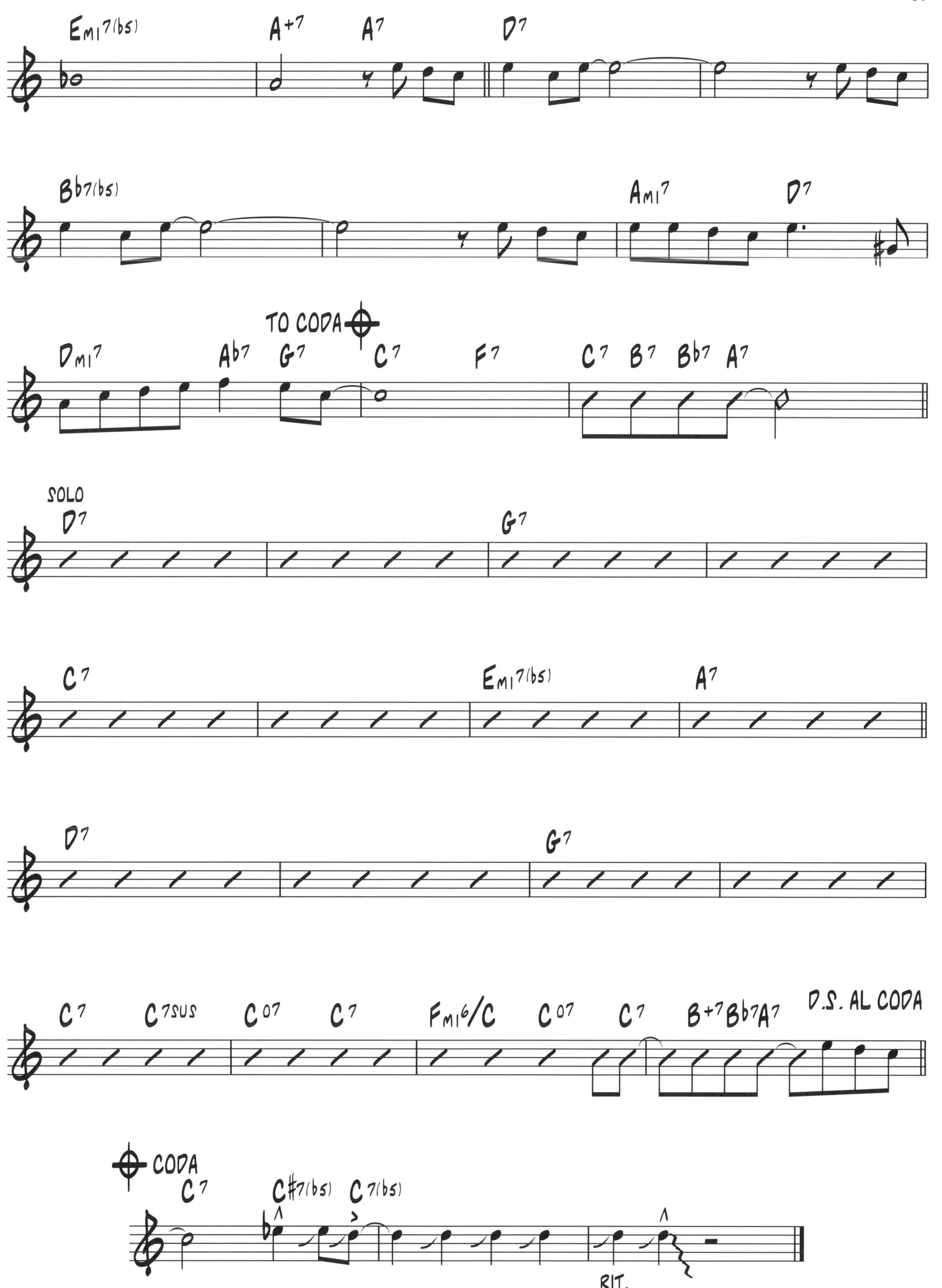
EMI7(b5)
A+7
A7
D7
Bb7(b5)
AMI7
D7
TO CODA
DMI7
Ab7
G7
C7
F7
C7
B7
Bb7
A7
SOLO
D7
G7
C7
EMI7(b5)
A7
D7
G7
C7
C7SUS
C07
C7
FMI6/C
C07
C7
B+7
Bb7
A7
D.S. AL CODA
CODA
C7
C#7(b5)
C7(b5)
RIT.

I WISH I DIDN'T LOVE YOU SO

FROM THE PARAMOUNT PICTURE THE PERILS OF PAULINE

WORDS AND MUSIC BY
FRANK LOESSER

B♭ VERSION

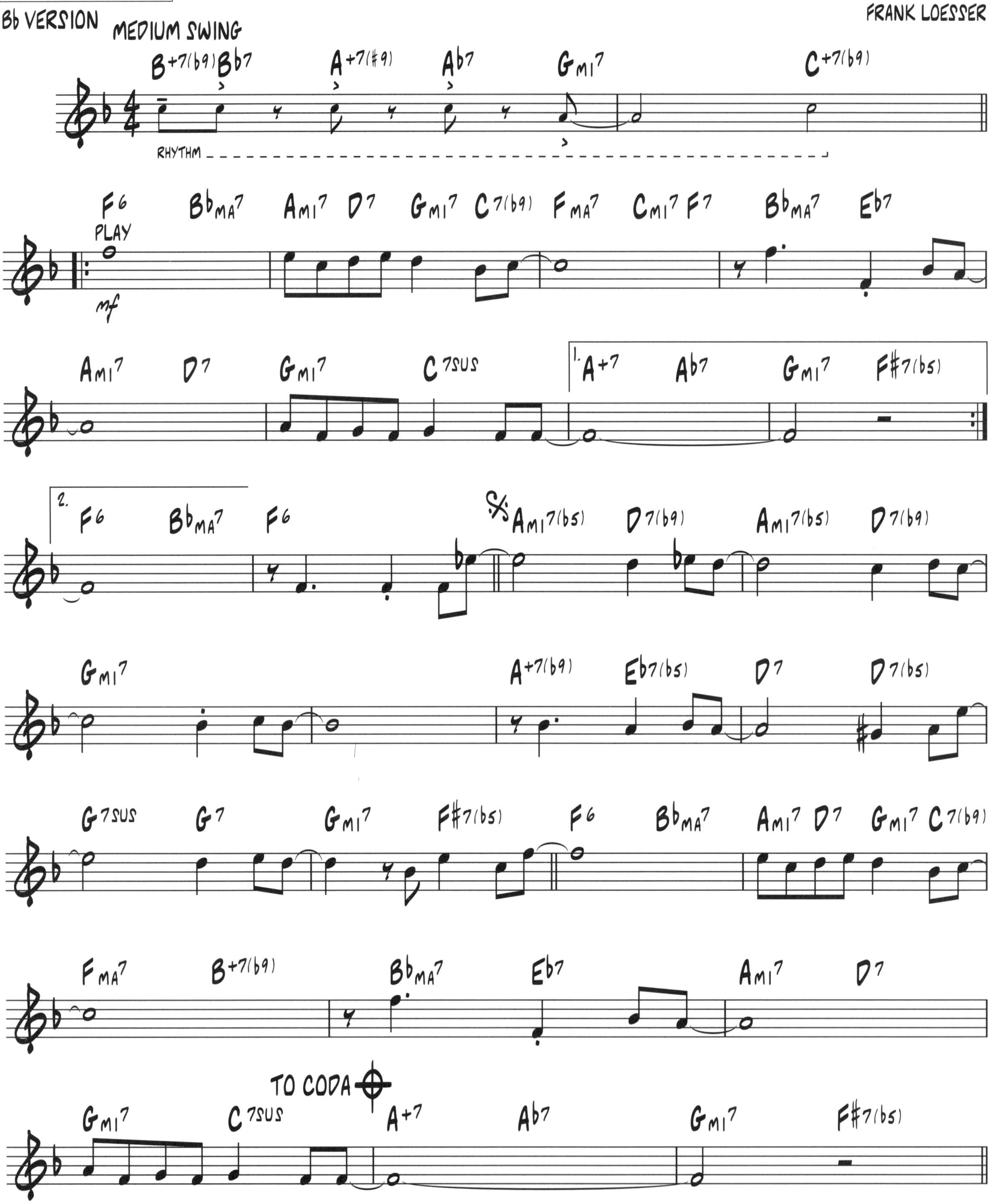

MEDIUM SWING

B+7(♭9) B♭7 A+7(♯9) A♭7 Gmi7 C+7(♭9)

RHYTHM

F6 B♭ma7 Ami7 D7 Gmi7 C7(♭9) Fma7 Cmi7 F7 B♭ma7 E♭7

PLAY *mf*

Ami7 D7 Gmi7 C7SUS 1. A+7 A♭7 Gmi7 F♯7(♭5)

2. F6 B♭ma7 F6 𝄋 Ami7(♭5) D7(♭9) Ami7(♭5) D7(♭9)

Gmi7 A+7(♭9) E♭7(♭5) D7 D7(♭5)

G7SUS G7 Gmi7 F♯7(♭5) F6 B♭ma7 Ami7 D7 Gmi7 C7(♭9)

Fma7 B+7(♭9) B♭ma7 E♭7 Ami7 D7

TO CODA 𝄌

Gmi7 C7SUS A+7 A♭7 Gmi7 F♯7(♭5)

SOLO
F6 Bbma7 Ami7 D7 Gmi7 C7(b9) Fma7 Cmi7 F7 Bbma7 Eb7
Ami7 D7 Gmi7 C7sus A+7 Ab7 Gmi7 F#7(b5)
F6 Bbma7 Ami7 D7 Gmi7 C7(b9) Fma7 B+7(b9) Bbma7 Eb7
Ami7 D7 Gmi7 C7sus F6 Bbma7 F6
Ami7(b5) D7(b9) Ami7(b5) D7(b9) Gmi7
A+7(b9) Eb7(b5) D7 D7(b5) G7sus G7 Gmi7 F#7(b5)
F6 Bbma7 Ami7 D7 Gmi7 C7(b9) Fma7 B+7(b9) Bbma7 Eb7
Ami7 D7 Gmi7 C7sus F6 Bbma7 F6
D.S. AL CODA
CODA
Bbma7 Eb7 Ab7 Db7 Gmi7 F#7(b5) Fma7

I'LL TAKE ROMANCE

LYRICS BY OSCAR HAMMERSTEIN II
MUSIC BY BEN OAKLAND

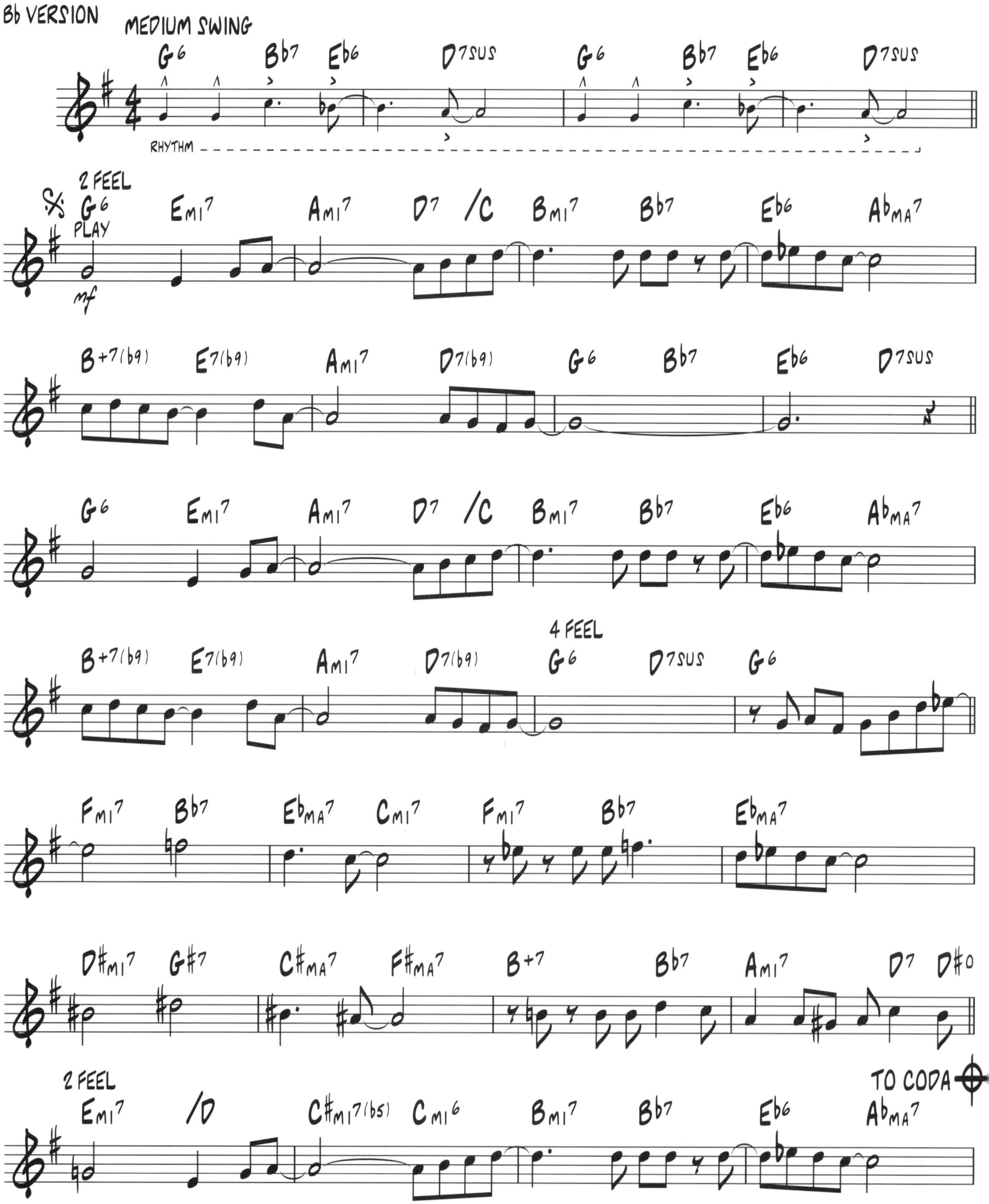

B♭ VERSION

MEDIUM SWING

G6 B♭7 E♭6 D7SUS G6 B♭7 E♭6 D7SUS

RHYTHM

2 FEEL

G6 Emi7 Ami7 D7 /C Bmi7 B♭7 E♭6 A♭ma7

PLAY

mf

B+7(♭9) E7(♭9) Ami7 D7(♭9) G6 B♭7 E♭6 D7SUS

G6 Emi7 Ami7 D7 /C Bmi7 B♭7 E♭6 A♭ma7

4 FEEL

B+7(♭9) E7(♭9) Ami7 D7(♭9) G6 D7SUS G6

Fmi7 B♭7 E♭ma7 Cmi7 Fmi7 B♭7 E♭ma7

D♯mi7 G♯7 C♯ma7 F♯ma7 B+7 B♭7 Ami7 D7 D♯o

2 FEEL

TO CODA

Emi7 /D C♯mi7(♭5) Cmi6 Bmi7 B♭7 E♭6 A♭ma7

B+7(b9) E7(b9) AMI7 D7(b9) G6
SOLO BREAK
SOLOS (2 CHORUSES)
4 FEEL
G6 EMI7 AMI7 D7 /C BMI7 Bb7 Eb6 AbMA7 B+7(b9) E7(b9)
AMI7 D7(b9) G6 Bb7 Eb6 D7 G6 EMI7 AMI7 D7 /C
BMI7 Bb7 Eb6 AbMA7 B+7(b9) E7(b9) AMI7 D7(b9) G6 D7SUS G6
FMI7 Bb7 EbMA7 CMI7 FMI7 Bb7 EbMA7 D#MI7 G#7 C#MA7 F#MA7
B+7 Bb7 EbMA7 D7 D#o EMI7 /D C#MI7(b5) CMI6 BMI7 Bb7
D.S. AL CODA
Eb6 AbMA7 B+7(b9) E7(b9) AMI7 D7(b9) G6 Bb7 Eb6 D7
CODA
B+7(b9) E7(b9) AMI7 D7(b9) G6 Bb7 Eb6 D7SUS
G6 Bb7 Eb6 D7SUS AbMA7 GMA7

CD #2

3 : SPLIT TRACK/MELODY
4 : FULL STEREO TRACK

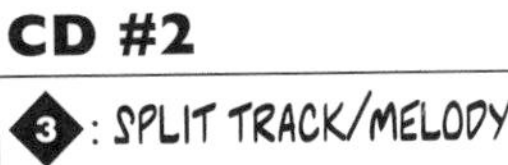

B♭ VERSION

IN THE WEE SMALL HOURS OF THE MORNING

WORDS BY BOB HILLIARD
MUSIC BY DAVID MANN

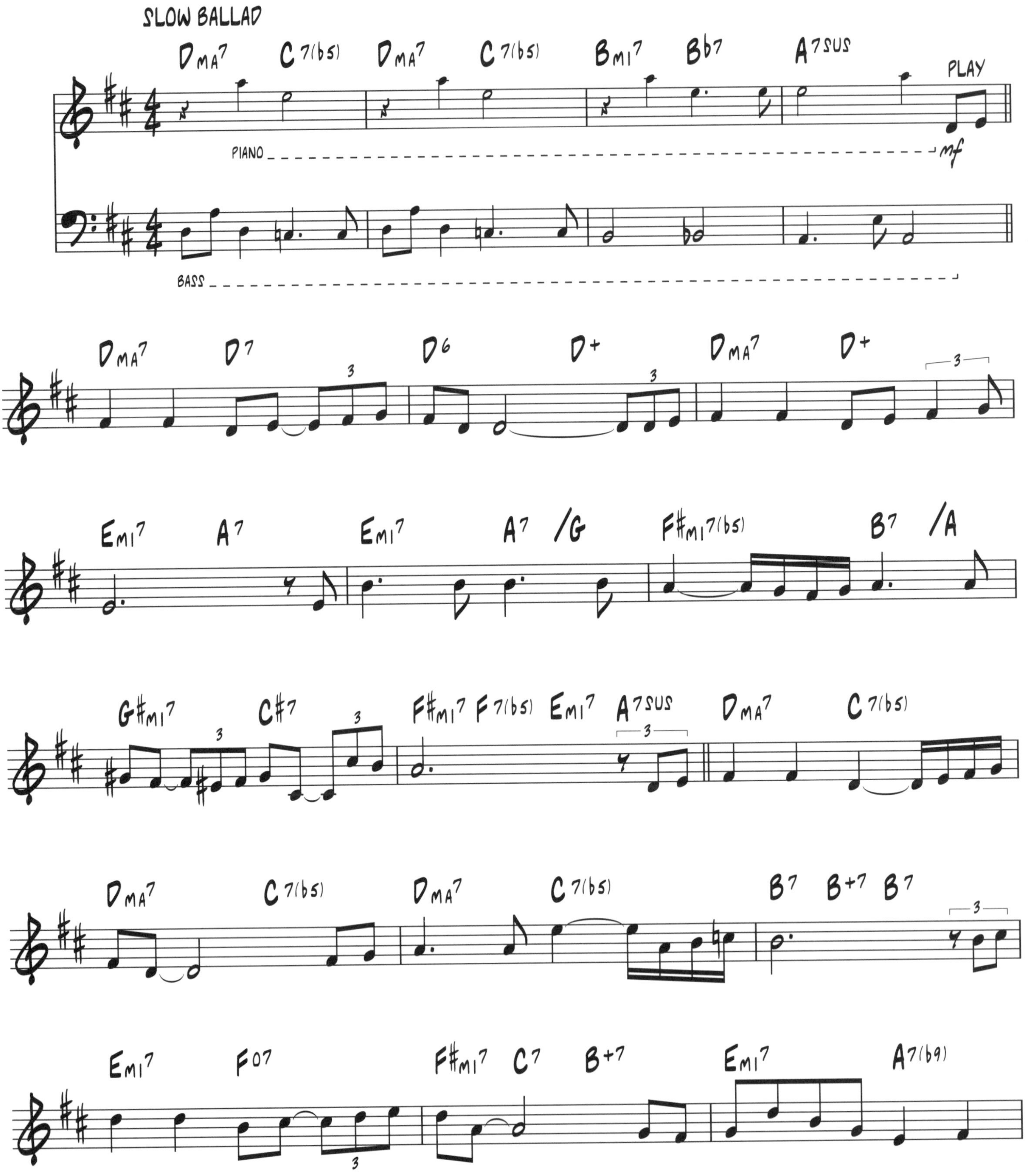
SLOW BALLAD
DMA7 C7(b5) DMA7 C7(b5) BMI7 Bb7 A7SUS
PLAY
PIANO
mf
BASS
DMA7 D7 D6 D+ DMA7 D+
EMI7 A7 EMI7 A7 /G F#MI7(b5) B7 /A
G#MI7 C#7 F#MI7 F7(b5) EMI7 A7SUS DMA7 C7(b5)
DMA7 C7(b5) DMA7 C7(b5) B7 B+7 B7
EMI7 F07 F#MI7 C7 B+7 EMI7 A7(b9)

D6 Eb7(b5)
SOLO
DMA7 D7 D6 D+
DMA7 D+ EMI7 A7 EMI7 A7 /G
F#MI7(b5) B7 /A G#MI7 C#7 F#MI7 F7(b5) EMI7 A7SUS
DMA7 C7(b5) DMA7 C7(b5) DMA7 C7(b5)
B7 B+7 B7 EMI7 F07 F#MI7 C7 B+7
3
3
EMI7 A7 /G F#MI7 B+7 EMI7 A7(b9)
GMA7 F6 EMI7 EbMA7 DMA7
RIT.

CD #2

5: SPLIT TRACK/MELODY
6: FULL STEREO TRACK

JUST IN TIME

FROM BELLS ARE RINGING

WORDS BY BETTY COMDEN AND ADOLPH GREEN
MUSIC BY JULE STYNE

Bb VERSION

MEDIUM SWING

G7 Bb7 B7 C7 Eb7(b5) Dmi7 G7(b9)
RHYTHM

CMA7 PLAY mf Bmi7 E7(#9)

A7SUS A7(b9) D7 C6/E F° D7/F#

G7SUS G7(b9) C7

FMA7 B+7(b9) BbMA7 Bmi7 E7(b9)

Ami Ami/G# Ami/G F#mi7(b5) B+7(b9)

C6 B7(b9) Bb7 A7

D7 G7SUS G7 C6 F7 Emi7 Eb7(b5)

TO CODA
D7 G7SUS G7(b9) C6
SOLO BREAK
SOLO
CMA7 BMI7 E7(#9) A7SUS A7(b9)
D7 C6/E F° D7/F# G7 G7(b9) C7
FMA7 BbMA7 BMI7 E7(b9) AMI
AMI/G# AMI/G F#MI7(b5) B+7(b9) C6 B7(b9)
Bb7 A7 D7 G7 C6 F7
D.S. AL CODA
EMI7 Eb7(b5) D7 G7 G7(b9) C6 Eb7(b5) DMI7 G7(b9)
CODA
F#7(b5) F7 E+7(#9) Eb7(b5) D7 Db7(b5) C7(b5)

CD #2

LIKE SOMEONE IN LOVE

WORDS BY JOHNNY BURKE
MUSIC BY JIMMY VAN HEUSEN

B♭ VERSION

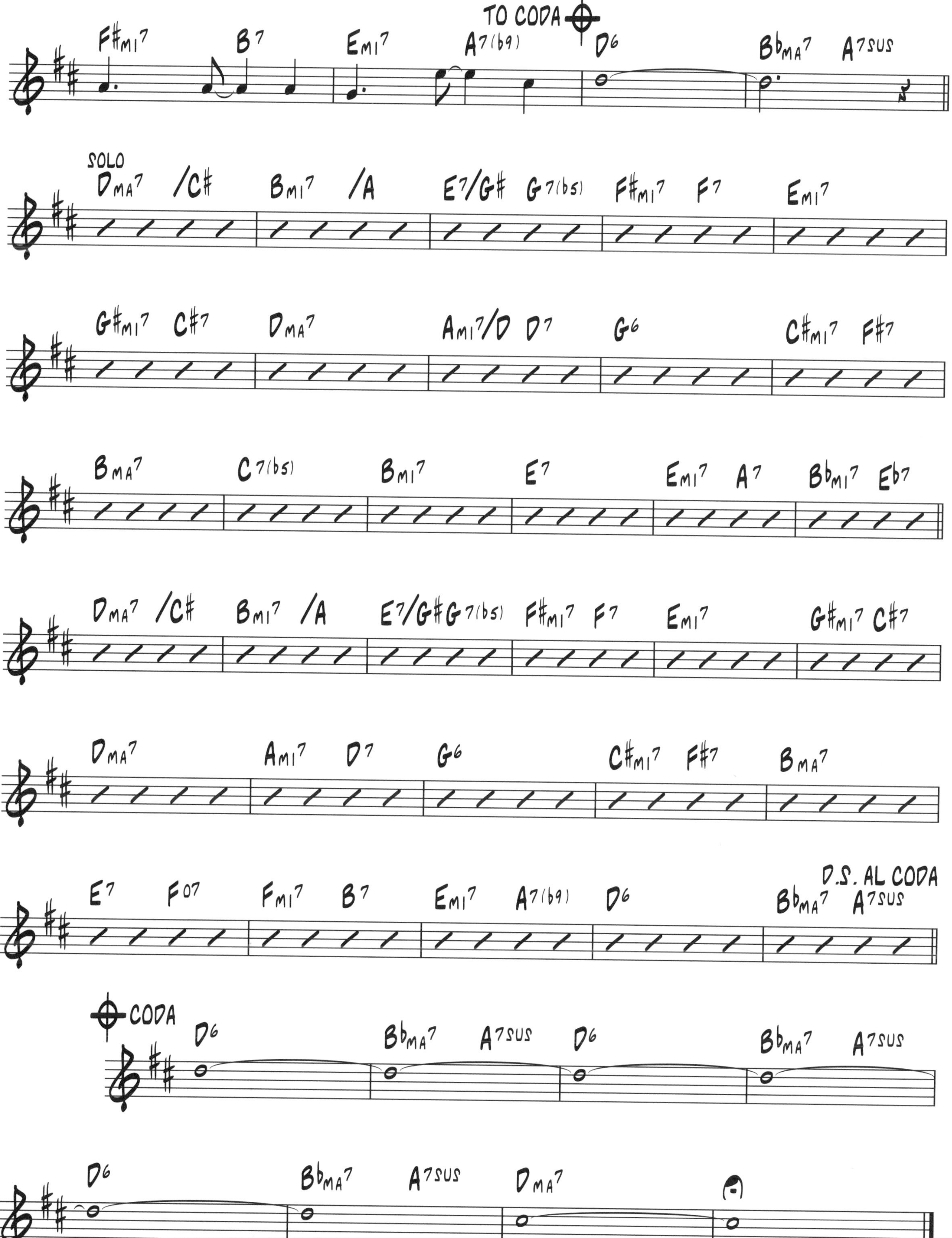
TO CODA
F#MI7 B7 EMI7 A7(b9) D6 BbMA7 A7SUS
SOLO
DMA7 /C# BMI7 /A E7/G# G7(b5) F#MI7 F7 EMI7
G#MI7 C#7 DMA7 AMI7/D D7 G6 C#MI7 F#7
BMA7 C7(b5) BMI7 E7 EMI7 A7 BbMI7 Eb7
DMA7 /C# BMI7 /A E7/G# G7(b5) F#MI7 F7 EMI7 G#MI7 C#7
DMA7 AMI7 D7 G6 C#MI7 F#7 BMA7
D.S. AL CODA
E7 F07 FMI7 B7 EMI7 A7(b9) D6 BbMA7 A7SUS
CODA
D6 BbMA7 A7SUS D6 BbMA7 A7SUS
D6 BbMA7 A7SUS DMA7

CD #2

9: SPLIT TRACK/MELODY

10: FULL STEREO TRACK

LOLLIPOPS AND ROSES

WORDS AND MUSIC BY
TONY VELONA

EMI7 A7(b9) AMI7 D7SUS Bb7 AMI7
D7 /C BMI7 EMI7 F°7 F#MI7(b5)
BMI7 E+7(#9) AMI7 D7(b9) GMA7
TO CODA
F7 /Eb G6/D D7SUS G6/D B+7 Bb7
SOLO
AMI7 D7 /C BMI7 EMI7 F°7 F#MI7(b5)
BMI7 E+7(#9) AMI7 D7(b9) GMA7 F7 /Eb
G6/D D7SUS G6/D
1.
BMI7 Bb7
2.
D.S. AL CODA
BMI7 E7(#9)
CODA
G6/D D7SUS G6/D E7(#9)
AMI7 D7SUS AMI7 AbMA7 GMA7

CD #2

11 : SPLIT TRACK/MELODY
12 : FULL STEREO TRACK

LOVE IS JUST AROUND THE CORNER

FROM THE PARAMOUNT PICTURE HERE IS MY HEART

WORDS AND MUSIC BY LEO ROBIN
AND LEWIS E. GENSLER

Bb VERSION

SOLOS (2 CHORUSES)
A7/C# D7/C G6/B E+7(b9) A7/C# D7/C G6/B E+7(b9)
A7/C# D7/C G6/B Bb7 A7 D7(b9) G6 Bb7/D
A7/C# D7/C G6/B E+7(b9) A7/C# D7/C G6/B E+7(b9)
A7/C# D7/C G6/B Bb7 A7 D7(b9) G6 F#MI7 B+7(b9)
EMI7 C#7(#9) F#MI7 B+7(b9) EMI7 A7 F#MI7 B7
EMI7 A7 AMI7 D7(b9) A7/C# D7/C G6/B E+7(b9) A7/C# D7/C
G6/B E+7(b9) A7/C# D7/C G6/B Bb7 A7 D7(b9) G6
D.S. AL CODA
CODA
A7 D7SUS D7(b9) G6 Bb7 A7 D7SUS D7(b9) G6 E+7(#9)
A7 D7SUS D7(b9) G6 C7 B7 Bb7 A7(b5) Ab7(b5) GMA7(b5)

CD #2

13 : SPLIT TRACK/MELODY
14 : FULL STEREO TRACK

B♭ VERSION

MY IDEAL

FROM THE PARAMOUNT PICTURE PLAYBOY OF PARIS

WORDS BY LEO ROBIN
MUSIC BY RICHARD A. WHITING AND NEWELL CHASE

TO CODA
FMA7 Bb7(b5) F6/A Ab7(b5) G7 C7(b9) F6 F#MA7
3
SOLO
F6 D7 GMI7 /F Eb7 D7 G7
C7 GMI7 C7(b9) FMA7 EMI7 A+7 DMI7 G7
G#MI7 /C# GMI7 F#7(b5) F6 D7 GMI7 /F
Eb7 D7 G7 GMI7 BbMI7 Eb7
D.S. AL CODA
FMA7 Bb7(b5) F6/A Ab7(b5) G7 C7(b9) F6 GMI7 C7(b9)
CODA
F6 F#MA7 F6 F#MA7 F6 F#7(b5) FMA7
RIT.

CD #2

15 : SPLIT TRACK/MELODY
16 : FULL STEREO TRACK

B♭ VERSION

ON A SLOW BOAT TO CHINA

BY FRANK LOESSER

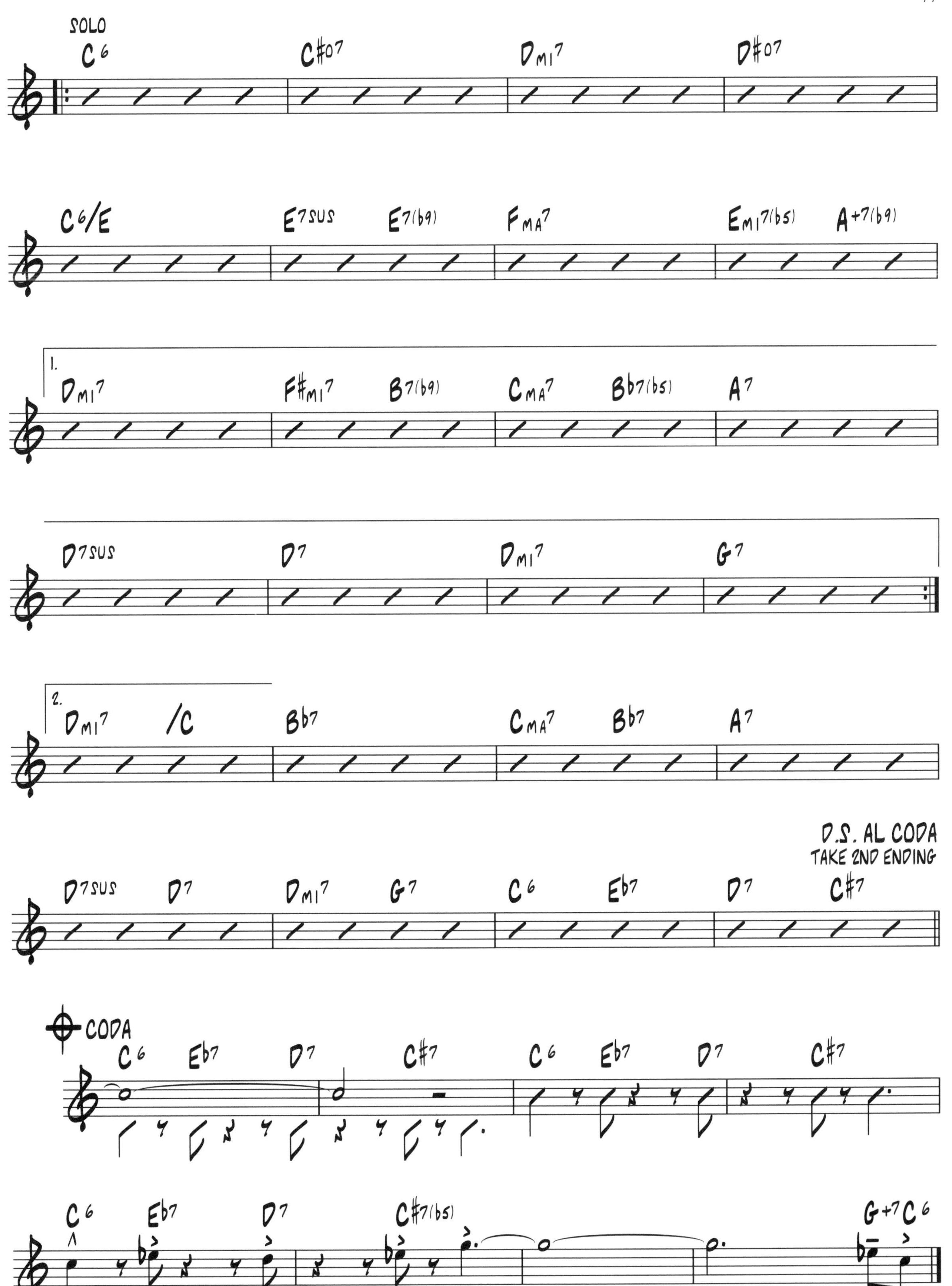
SOLO
C6
C#o7
Dmi7
D#o7
C6/E
E7sus
E7(b9)
Fma7
Emi7(b5)
A+7(b9)
1.
Dmi7
F#mi7
B7(b9)
Cma7
Bb7(b5)
A7
D7sus
D7
Dmi7
G7
2.
Dmi7
/C
Bb7
Cma7
Bb7
A7
D.S. AL CODA
TAKE 2ND ENDING
D7sus
D7
Dmi7
G7
C6
Eb7
D7
C#7
CODA
C6
Eb7
D7
C#7
C6
Eb7
D7
C#7
C6
Eb7
D7
C#7(b5)
G+7
C6

CD #2

17 : SPLIT TRACK/MELODY
18 : FULL STEREO TRACK

TOO LATE NOW

FROM ROYAL WEDDING

WORDS BY ALAN JAY LERNER
MUSIC BY BURTON LANE

B♭ VERSION

DMA7 /C# BMI7 EMI7 A7SUS DMA7 /C# BMI7
EMI7 A7SUS DMA7 /C# BMI7 /A G#MI7(b5) G7(b5)
TO CODA
F#MI7 F7 EMI7 A7 D6 EbMA7
SOLO
DMA7 BMI7 EMI7 A7SUS DMA7 BMI7
EMI7 A7SUS DMA7 BMI7
1.
G#MI7(b5) C#+7 F#MI7 F7 EMI7 A7
2.
G#MI7(b5) G7(b5) F#MI7 F7 EMI7 A7 D6 C#MI7 F#+7
BMI6 C#MI7 F#7 BMI7 E+7 AMI6
BMI7 E7(b9) EMI7 A7 DMA7 BMI7 EMI7 A7SUS DMA7 BMI7
EMI7 A7SUS DMA7 BMI7 G#MI7(b5) G7(b5) F#MI7 F7 EMI7 A7 D6
D.S. AL CODA
CODA
F#MI7 F7 EMI7 A7 Bb6 C6 D6
RIT.

CD #2

19 : SPLIT TRACK/MELODY

20 : FULL STEREO TRACK

YOU ARE TOO BEAUTIFUL

FROM HALLELUJAH, I'M A BUM

WORDS BY LORENZ HART
MUSIC BY RICHARD RODGERS

B♭ VERSION

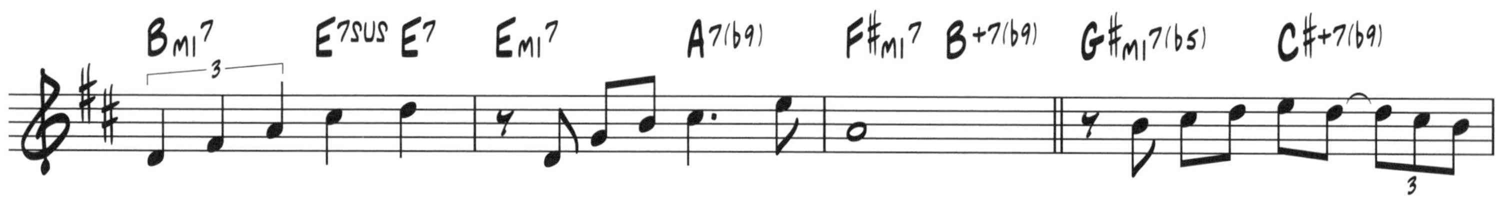

C♯MI7(♭5) F♯7(♭9) BMI7 E7SUS E7 B♭7(♭5) A7 A7(♭9)
G♯MI7(♭5) C♯+7(♭9) F♯MI7 B+7(♭9) EMI7 A+7(♭9)
DMA7 AMI7 D7(♭9) GMA7 C7 BMI7 E7SUS E7
TO CODA
SOLO
E7 E+7 A7SUS A7(♭9) D6 F♯MI7 B+7(♭9) G♯MI7(♭5) C♯+7(♭9) F♯MI7 B+7(♭9)
EMI7 A+7(♭9) DMA7 AMI7 D7(♭9) GMA7 C7 BMI7 E7SUS E7
D.S. AL CODA
1. EMI7 A7(♭9) F♯MI7 B+7(♭9)
2. E7 E+7 A7SUS A7(♭9) D6 AMI7 D7
CODA B♭MA7 E♭MA7 DMA7
RIT.

CD #1

1: SPLIT TRACK/MELODY
2: FULL STEREO TRACK

ALL THE THINGS YOU ARE

FROM VERY WARM FOR MAY

LYRICS BY OSCAR HAMMERSTEIN II
MUSIC BY JEROME KERN

Eb VERSION

BbMA7 Eb7 AMI7 G#o7
GMI7 C7 TO CODA F6 EMI7(b5) A7(b9)
SOLOS (2 CHORUSES)
DMI7 GMI7 C7 FMA7 BbMA7
BMI7 E7 AMA7 AMI7 DMI7
G7 CMA7 FMA7 F#MI7(b5) B7 EMA7
F#MI7 B7 EMA7
D#MI7(b5) G#7 C#MA7 A+7(b9) DMI7
GMI7 C7 FMA7 BbMA7 Eb7
D.S. AL CODA
AMI7 G#o7 GMI7 C7 F6 EMI7(b5) A7(b9)
CODA
N.C. Bb7(#9)
1ST X ONLY
1. A7(#9)
2. A7(#9)

CD #1

3: SPLIT TRACK/MELODY
4: FULL STEREO TRACK

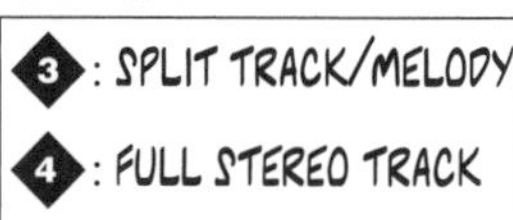

ALMOST LIKE BEING IN LOVE

FROM BRIGADOON

LYRICS BY ALAN JAY LERNER
MUSIC BY FREDERICK LOEWE

E♭ VERSION

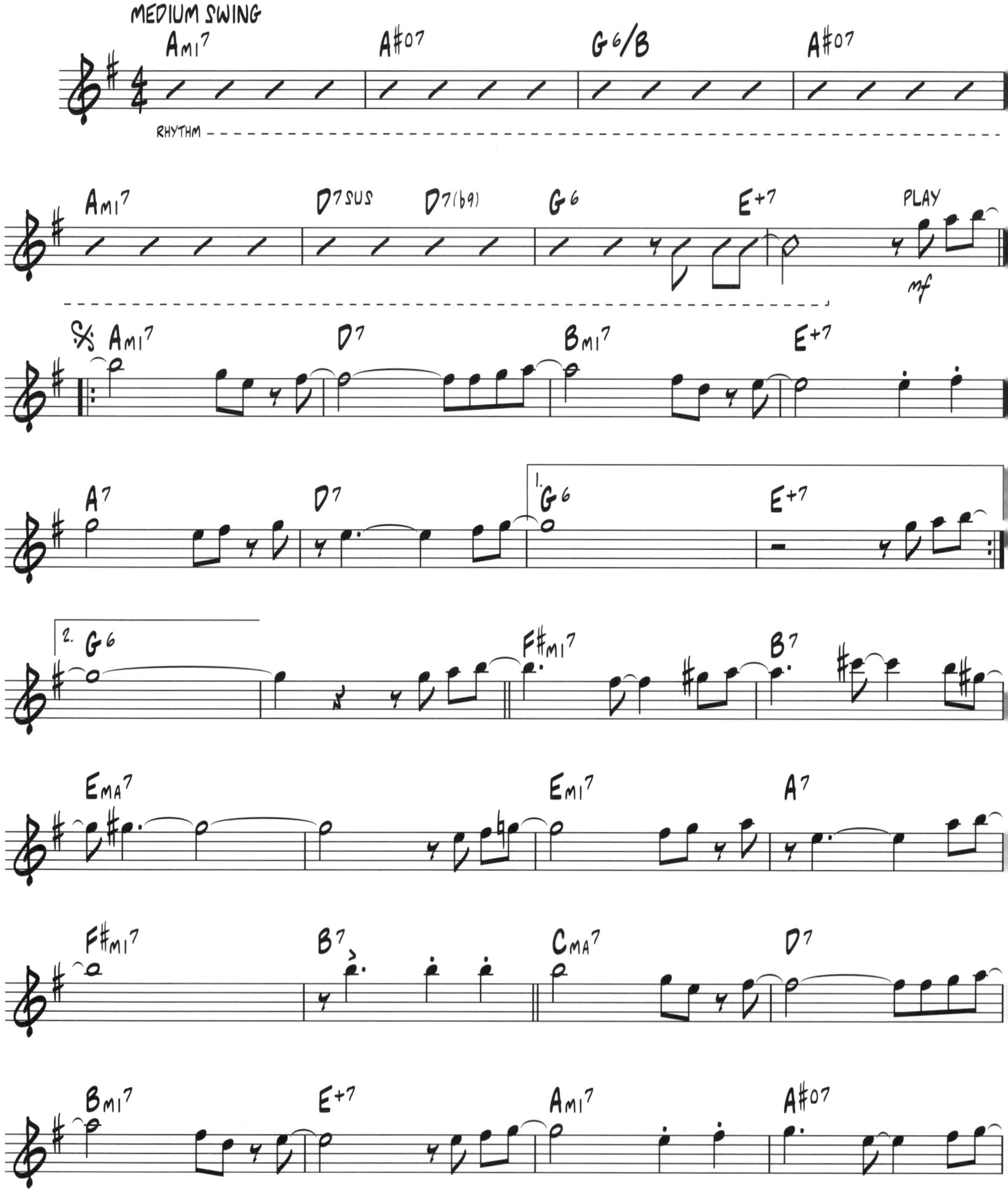
MEDIUM SWING
AMI7 A#O7 G6/B A#O7
RHYTHM
AMI7 D7SUS D7(♭9) G6 E+7
PLAY
mf
AMI7 D7 BMI7 E+7
A7 D7
1. G6 E+7
2. G6 F#MI7 B7
EMA7 EMI7 A7
F#MI7 B7 CMA7 D7
BMI7 E+7 AMI7 A#O7

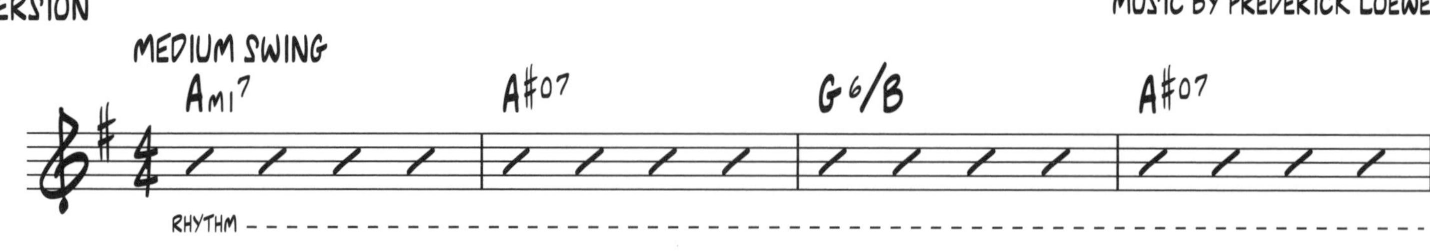

TO CODA
G6/B
A#o7
Ami7
D7sus
D7(b9)
G6
SOLO BREAK
SOLOS (2 CHORUSES)
Ami7
D7
Bmi7
E+7
A7
D7
G6
E+7
Ami7
D7
Bmi7
E+7
A7
D7
G6
F#mi7
B7
Ema7
Emi7
A7
F#mi7
B7
Cma7
D7
Bmi7
E+7
Ami7
A#o7
G6/B
A#o7
Ami7
D7sus
D7(b9)
G6
E+7
D.S. AL CODA
TAKE REPEAT
LAST X ONLY
CODA
D7sus
D7(b9)
C#7(b5)
C7
B+7(#9)
Bb7(b5)
Ami7
G#ma7
Gma7

CD #1

5: SPLIT TRACK/MELODY
6: FULL STEREO TRACK

BLUE SKIES

FROM BETSY

WORDS AND MUSIC BY
IRVING BERLIN

E♭ VERSION

MEDIUM SALSA

D#MI7 G#7(#9)

RHYTHM

C#MI PLAY *mf* G#7(b9)/C E/B A#MI7(b5)

E/B C#7(#9) F#MI7 B7 1. EMA7 A7 D#MI7 G#7(b9)

2. EMA7 D7 D#7 E7 F7 E7 D7

E7 A7 D7 E7 F7

E7 D7 E7 D#+7(#9) A7 G#7(#9)

C#MI G#7(b9)/C E/B A#MI7(b5) TO CODA

E/B C#7(#9) F#MI7 B7 EMA7 F#MI7 B7(#9) CMI7

SOLOS (2 FULL CHORUSES)
C#MI G#7(b9)/C E/B A#MI7(b5) E/B C#7(#9)
F#MI7 B7 1. EMA7 A7 D#MI7 G#7(b9) 2. EMA7 D7 D#7
E7 F7 E7 D7 E7 A7 B7
E7 F7 E7 D7 E7 D#7 G#7
C#MI G#7(b9)/C E/B A#MI7(b5)
D.S. AL CODA
TAKE REPEAT
E/B C#7(#9) F#MI7 B7 EMA7 F#MI7 B7(#9) CMI7
CODA E/B C#7(#9) F#MI7 B7 EMA7 C#7(#9) F#MI7 B7(b9)
EMA7 C#7(#9) F#MI7 B7 EMA7 G7 C7 F7
3
EMA7 C#7(#9) F#MI7 B7 EMA7 D7 D#7 E6

CD #1

9: SPLIT TRACK/MELODY

10: FULL STEREO TRACK

COME RAIN OR COME SHINE

FROM ST. LOUIS WOMAN

WORDS BY JOHNNY MERCER
MUSIC BY HAROLD ARLEN

Eb VERSION

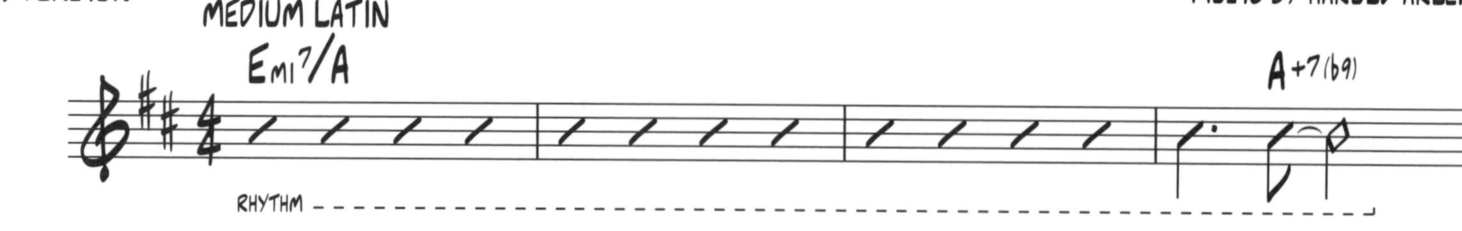

TO CODA
BMI7 G#+7(#9) G7(b5) F#7(b9) B7(#9) E7 E+7 A7SUS A7(b9)
SOLO
DMA7 C#MI7 F#+7 BMI7
E7SUS E+7 A7SUS A7(b9) DMA7 Bb7 AMI7 G#7(b5)
GMI7 DMI6 G#7(b5) GMI7 F7 EMI7(b5) A7(b9)
G#MI7(b5) C#7(b9) F#MI7(b5) B7(b9) F#MI7(b5) B+7(b9) E7 A7SUS A7(b9)
DMA7 C#MI7 F#+7 BMI7 C7(b5) BMI7
FMI7 Bb7 D#MI7 G#+7 C#MI7 F#+7 C#MI7 C7(b5)
B7SUS C#MI7 Do7 B7/D# E7SUS F#MI7 GMA7 F#+7 F#7(b9)
D.S. AL CODA
BMI7 G#+7(#9) G7(b5) F#7(b9) B7(#9) E7 E+7 A7SUS A7(b9)
CODA
4X'S
B7(#9) E7 F#+7 BMI7
1ST X ONLY
RIT. LAST TIME

CD #1

11: SPLIT TRACK/MELODY
12: FULL STEREO TRACK

DESAFINADO

E♭ VERSION

ORIGINAL TEXT BY NEWTON MENDONÇA
MUSIC BY ANTONIO CARLOS JOBIM

B7(b9) E7SUS E+7 A7SUS A7(b9) DMA7
E7(b5) EMI7 A7 F#MI7(b5)
B+7(#9) B7(b9) EMI7 C7 DMA7 F0
E7SUS E7 E7SUS E7 C7SUS C7 C7SUS C7 E7SUS E7
TO CODA
SOLO
EMI7 A7 DMA7 Eb7(b5) DMA7 E7(b5)
EMI7 A7 F#MI7(b5) B7(b9) EMI7 C#MI7(b5) F#7(b9) 1. BMA7
B7(b9) E7 E7(b9) EbMA7 Eb7(b5) 2. BMI7 C#7
F#MA7 F+7 E7 Eb7 F#MA7 G0 G#MI7
C#7 F#MA7 D#MI7 G#MI7 C#7 AMA7
D.S. AL CODA
A#0 BMI7 E7 EMI7 B7(b9) EMI7 A7
CODA
DMA7 Eb7(b5) DMA7 Eb7(b5)
3
DMA7 Eb7(b5) DMA7

CD #1
13: SPLIT TRACK/MELODY
14: FULL STEREO TRACK

DON'T GET AROUND MUCH ANYMORE

FROM SOPHISTICATED LADY

E♭ VERSION

WORDS AND MUSIC BY DUKE ELLINGTON
AND BOB RUSSELL

SOLO
AMA7
F#7
B7
E7
1.
AMA7
BMI7
E7
2.
AMA7
F7
EMI7
A7
DMA7
D#07
AMA7/E
A7
DMA7
D#07
G#7(b9)
C#MI7
C07
BMI7
E7
AMA7
F#7
B7
E7
AMA7
N.C. /E
D.S. AL CODA
TAKE REPEAT
CODA
AMA7
E7
RHYTHM
AMA7
E7
RHYTHM
AMA7
F7
E7
A6
RHYTHM

CD #1

15 : SPLIT TRACK/MELODY

16 : FULL STEREO TRACK

FOR ALL WE KNOW

FROM THE MOTION PICTURE LOVERS AND OTHER STRANGERS

WORDS BY ROBB WILSON AND ARTHUR JAMES
MUSIC BY FRED KARLIN

Eb VERSION

TO CODA
DMI7 G#7(b5) G7SUS G7(b9) G#MA7 C#MA7(b5)
SOLO
C6 D7 D+7 G7 G7SUS G7(b9) CMA7 FMA7
EMI7 A+7(b9) DMI7 G#7(b5) G7SUS G7(b9) EMI7 Eb0
DMI7 G7 AMI7 /E Eb0 DMI7
G7SUS G7(b9) C6 D7 D+7 G7 G7SUS G7(b9)
CMA7 FMA7 EMI7 A+7(b9) DMI7 G#7(b5) G7SUS G7(b9)
CMA7 F7(b5) E7 Bb7(b5) A7SUS A7(b9)
DMI7 G#7(b5) G7SUS G7(b9) G#MA7 C#MA7(b5) D.S. AL CODA
CODA
G#MA7 C#MA7(b5) G#MA7 C#MA7(b5) CMA7(b5)
RHYTHM
RIT.

CD #1

17 : SPLIT TRACK/MELODY
18 : FULL STEREO TRACK

I GOTTA RIGHT TO SING THE BLUES

WORDS BY TED KOEHL
MUSIC BY HAROLD ARL

E♭ VERSION

SLOW BLUES

BMI7(b5) E+7 E7 A7

F7(b5) EMI7 A7

AMI7 Eb7 TO CODA D7 G7 C7 G7 F#7 F7 E7

SOLO
A7 D7

G7 BMI7(b5) E7

A7 D7

G7 G7SUS G07 G7 CMI6/G G07 G7 F#+7 F7 E7 D.S. AL CODA

CODA G7 G#7(b5) G7(b5)

RIT.

CD #1

19: SPLIT TRACK/MELODY
20: FULL STEREO TRACK

I WISH I DIDN'T LOVE YOU SO

FROM THE PARAMOUNT PICTURE THE PERILS OF PAULINE

WORDS AND MUSIC BY
FRANK LOESSER

E♭ VERSION

SOLO
C6 FMA7 EMI7 A7 DMI7 G7(b9) CMA7 GMI7 C7 FMA7 Bb7
EMI7 A7 DMI7 G7SUS E+7 Eb7 DMI7 C#7(b5)
C6 FMA7 EMI7 A7 DMI7 G7(b9) CMA7 F#+7(b9) FMA7 Bb7
EMI7 A7 DMI7 G7SUS C6 FMA7 C6
EMI7(b5) A7(b9) EMI7(b5) A7(b9) DMI7
E+7(b9) Bb7(b5) A7 A7(b5) D7SUS D7 DMI7 C#7(b5)
C6 FMA7 EMI7 A7 DMI7 G7(b9) CMA7 F#+7(b9) FMA7 Bb7
EMI7 A7 DMI7 G7SUS C6 FMA7 C6
D.S. AL CODA
CODA
FMA7 Bb7 Eb7 Ab7 DMI7 C#7(b5) CMA7

CD #2

I'LL TAKE ROMANCE

LYRICS BY OSCAR HAMMERSTEIN II
MUSIC BY BEN OAKLAND

F#+7(b9) B7(b9) Emi7 A7(b9) D6
SOLO BREAK
SOLOS (2 CHORUSES)
4 FEEL
D6 Bmi7 Emi7 A7 /G F#mi7 F7 Bb6 Ebma7 F#+7(b9) B7(b9)
Emi7 A7(b9) D6 F7 Bb6 A7 D6 Bmi7 Emi7 A7 /G
F#mi7 F7 Bb6 Ebma7 F#+7(b9) B7(b9) Emi7 A7(b9) D6 A7sus D6
Cmi7 F7 Bbma7 Gmi7 Cmi7 F7 Bbma7 A#mi7 D#7 G#ma7 C#ma7
F#+7 F7 Bbma7 A7 A#o Bmi7 /A G#mi7(b5) Gmi6 F#mi7 F7
D.S. AL CODA
Bb6 Ebma7 F#+7(b9) B7(b9) Emi7 A7(b9) D6 F7 Bb6 A7
CODA
F#+7(b9) B7(b9) Emi7 A7(b9) D6 F7 Bb6 A7sus
D6 F7 Bb6 A7sus Ebma7 Dma7

CD #2

3: SPLIT TRACK/MELODY

4: FULL STEREO TRACK

IN THE WEE SMALL HOURS OF THE MORNING

Eb VERSION

WORDS BY BOB HILLIARD
MUSIC BY DAVID MANN

SOLO
A6 Bb7(b5)
AMA7 A7 A6 A+
AMA7 A+ BMI7 E7 BMI7 E7 /D
C#MI7(b5) F#7 /E D#MI7 G#7 C#MI7 C7(b5) BMI7 E7SUS
AMA7 G7(b5) AMA7 G7(b5) AMA7 G7(b5)
F#7 F#+7 F#7 BMI7 C07 C#MI7 G7 F#+7
BMI7 E7 /D C#MI7 F#+7 BMI7 E7(b9)
DMA7 C6 BMI7 BbMA7 AMA7
RIT.

CD #2

5: SPLIT TRACK/MELODY
6: FULL STEREO TRACK

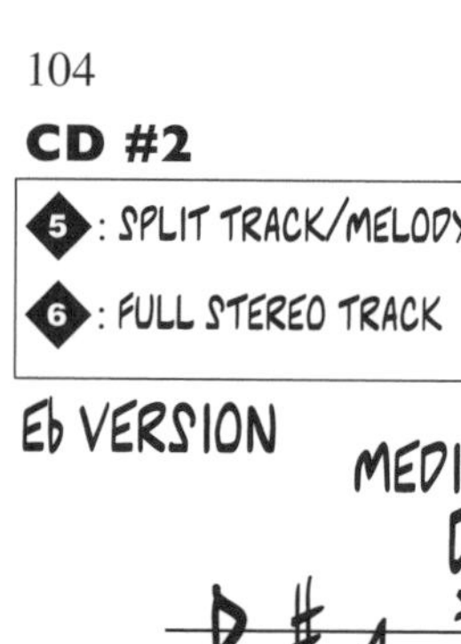

JUST IN TIME

FROM BELLS ARE RINGING

WORDS BY BETTY COMDEN AND ADOLPH GREEN
MUSIC BY JULE STYNE

Eb VERSION

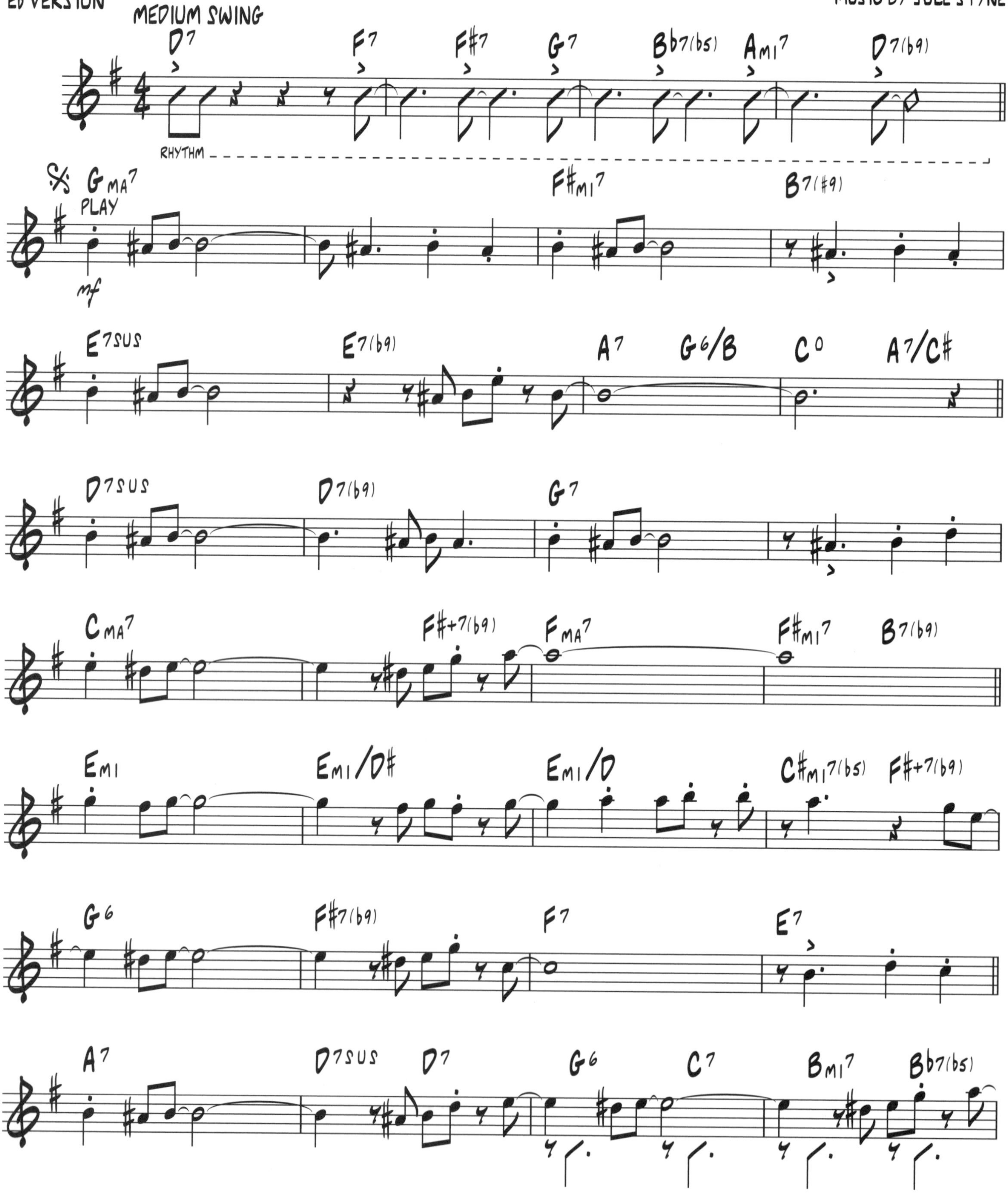
MEDIUM SWING
D7 F7 F#7 G7 Bb7(b5) AMI7 D7(b9)
RHYTHM
GMA7 F#MI7 B7(#9)
PLAY
mf
E7SUS E7(b9) A7 G6/B C° A7/C#
D7SUS D7(b9) G7
CMA7 F#+7(b9) FMA7 F#MI7 B7(b9)
EMI EMI/D# EMI/D C#MI7(b5) F#+7(b9)
G6 F#7(b9) F7 E7
A7 D7SUS D7 G6 C7 BMI7 Bb7(b5)

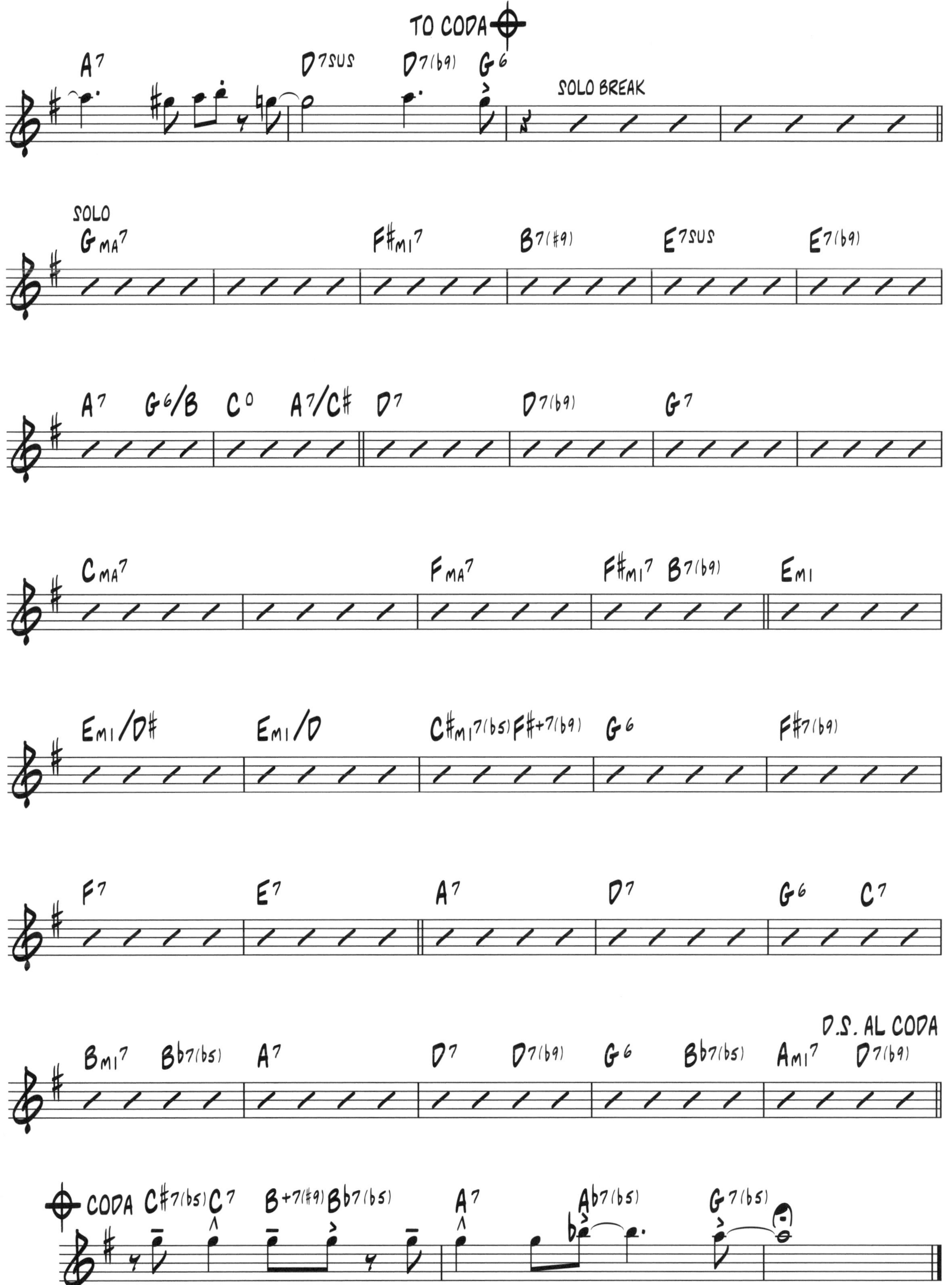
TO CODA
A7
D7SUS
D7(b9)
G6
SOLO BREAK
SOLO
GMA7
F#MI7
B7(#9)
E7SUS
E7(b9)
A7
G6/B
C0
A7/C#
D7
D7(b9)
G7
CMA7
FMA7
F#MI7
B7(b9)
EMI
EMI/D#
EMI/D
C#MI7(b5)
F#+7(b9)
G6
F#7(b9)
F7
E7
A7
D7
G6
C7
D.S. AL CODA
BMI7
Bb7(b5)
A7
D7
D7(b9)
G6
Bb7(b5)
AMI7
D7(b9)
CODA
C#7(b5)
C7
B+7(#9)
Bb7(b5)
A7
Ab7(b5)
G7(b5)

CD #2

7: SPLIT TRACK/MELODY
8: FULL STEREO TRACK

Eb VERSION

LIKE SOMEONE IN LOVE

WORDS BY JOHNNY BURKE
MUSIC BY JIMMY VAN HEUSEN

TO CODA
C#MI7
F#7
BMI7
E7(b9)
A6
FMA7
E7SUS
SOLO
AMA7 /G#
F#MI7 /E
B7/D# D7(b5)
C#MI7 C7
BMI7
D#MI7 G#7
AMA7
EMI7/A A7
D6
G#MI7 C#7
F#MA7
G7(b5)
F#MI7
B7
BMI7 E7
FMI7 Bb7
AMA7 /G#
F#MI7 /E
B7/D# D7(b5)
C#MI7 C7
BMI7
D#MI7 G#7
AMA7
EMI7 A7
D6
G#MI7 C#7
F#MA7
D.S. AL CODA
B7 C07
C#MI7 F#7
BMI7 E7(b9)
A6
FMA7 E7SUS
CODA
A6
FMA7 E7SUS
A6
FMA7 E7SUS
A6
FMA7 E7SUS
AMA7

CD #2

9 : SPLIT TRACK/MELODY
10 : FULL STEREO TRACK

LOLLIPOPS AND ROSES

WORDS AND MUSIC BY
TONY VELONA

BMI7 E7(b9) EMI7 A7SUS F7 EMI7
A7 /G F#MI7 BMI7 C07 C#MI7(b5)
F#MI7 B+7(#9) EMI7 A7(b9) DMA7
TO CODA
C7 /Bb D6/A A7SUS D6/A F#+7 F7
SOLO
EMI7 A7 /G F#MI7 BMI7 C07 C#MI7(b5)
F#MI7 B+7(#9) EMI7 A7(b9) DMA7 C7 /Bb
D6/A A7SUS D6/A
1. F#MI7 F7
2. D.S. AL CODA F#MI7 B7(#9)
CODA
D6/A A7SUS D6/A B7(#9)
EMI7 A7SUS EMI7 EbMA7 DMA7

CD #2

11 : SPLIT TRACK/MELODY
12 : FULL STEREO TRACK

LOVE IS JUST AROUND THE CORNER

FROM THE PARAMOUNT PICTURE HERE IS MY HEART

WORDS AND MUSIC BY LEO ROBIN
AND LEWIS E. GENSLER

Eb VERSION

MEDIUM SWING

E7/D A7/G D6/F# B+7(b9) E7/G# A7/G D6/F# B+7(b9)

RHYTHM

E7/G# A7/G D6/F# B+7(b9) E7/G# A7/G

PLAY

mf

D6/F# B+7(b9) E7/G# A7/G D6/F# F7

E7 A7SUS A7(b9) D6 1. F7 2.

4 FEEL

C#MI7 F#+7(b9) BMI7 G#7(#9) C#MI7 F#+7(b9) BMI7

BMI7 E7 C#MI7 F#7 BMI7 E7 EMI7 A7(b9)

2 FEEL

E7/G# A7/G D6/F# B+7(b9) E7/G# A7/G D6/F# B+7(b9)

TO CODA

E7/G# A7/G D6/F# F7 E7 A7SUS A7(b9) D6

SOLO BREAK

SOLOS (2 CHORUSES)
E7/G# A7/G D6/F# B+7(b9) E7/G# A7/G D6/F# B+7(b9)
E7/G# A7/G D6/F# F7 E7 A7(b9) D6 F7/A
E7/G# A7/G D6/F# B+7(b9) E7/G# A7/G D6/F# B+7(b9)
E7/G# A7/G D6/F# F7 E7 A7(b9) D6 C#MI7 F#+7(b9)
BMI7 G#7(#9) C#MI7 F#+7(b9) BMI7 E7 C#MI7 F#7
BMI7 E7 EMI7 A7(b9) E7/G# A7/G D6/F# B+7(b9) E7/G# A7/G
D6/F# B+7(b9) E7/G# A7/G D6/F# F7 E7 A7(b9) D6 D.S. AL CODA
CODA E7 A7SUS A7(b9) D6 F7 E7 A7SUS A7(b9) D6 B+7(#9)
E7 A7SUS A7(b9) D6 G7 F#7 F7 E7(b5) Eb7(b5) DMA7(b5)

CD #2

13: SPLIT TRACK/MELODY
14: FULL STEREO TRACK

Eb VERSION

MY IDEAL

FROM THE PARAMOUNT PICTURE PLAYBOY OF PARIS

WORDS BY LEO ROBIN
MUSIC BY RICHARD A. WHITING AND NEWELL CHASE

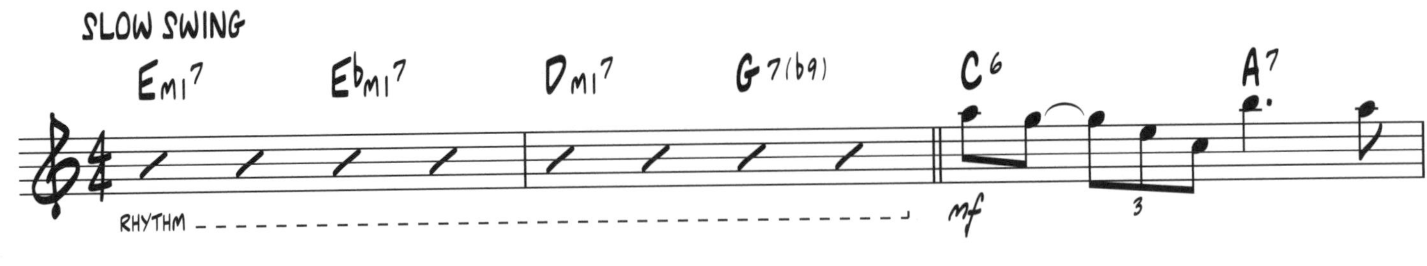

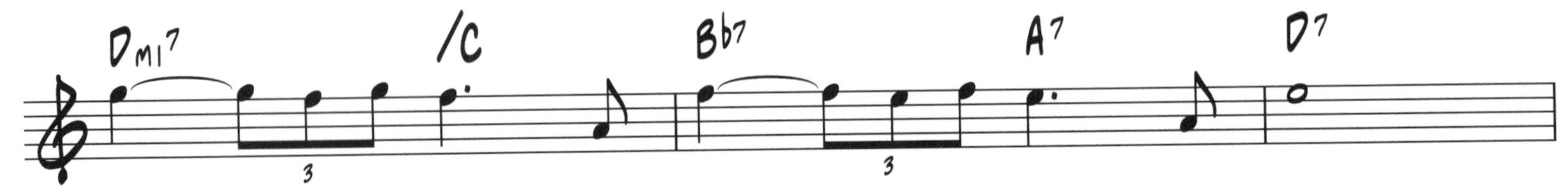

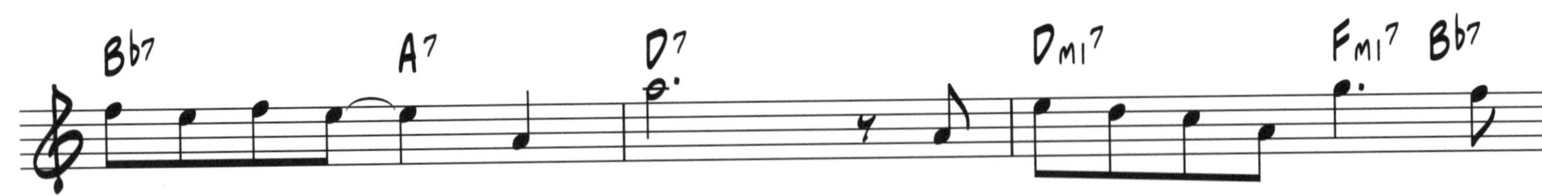

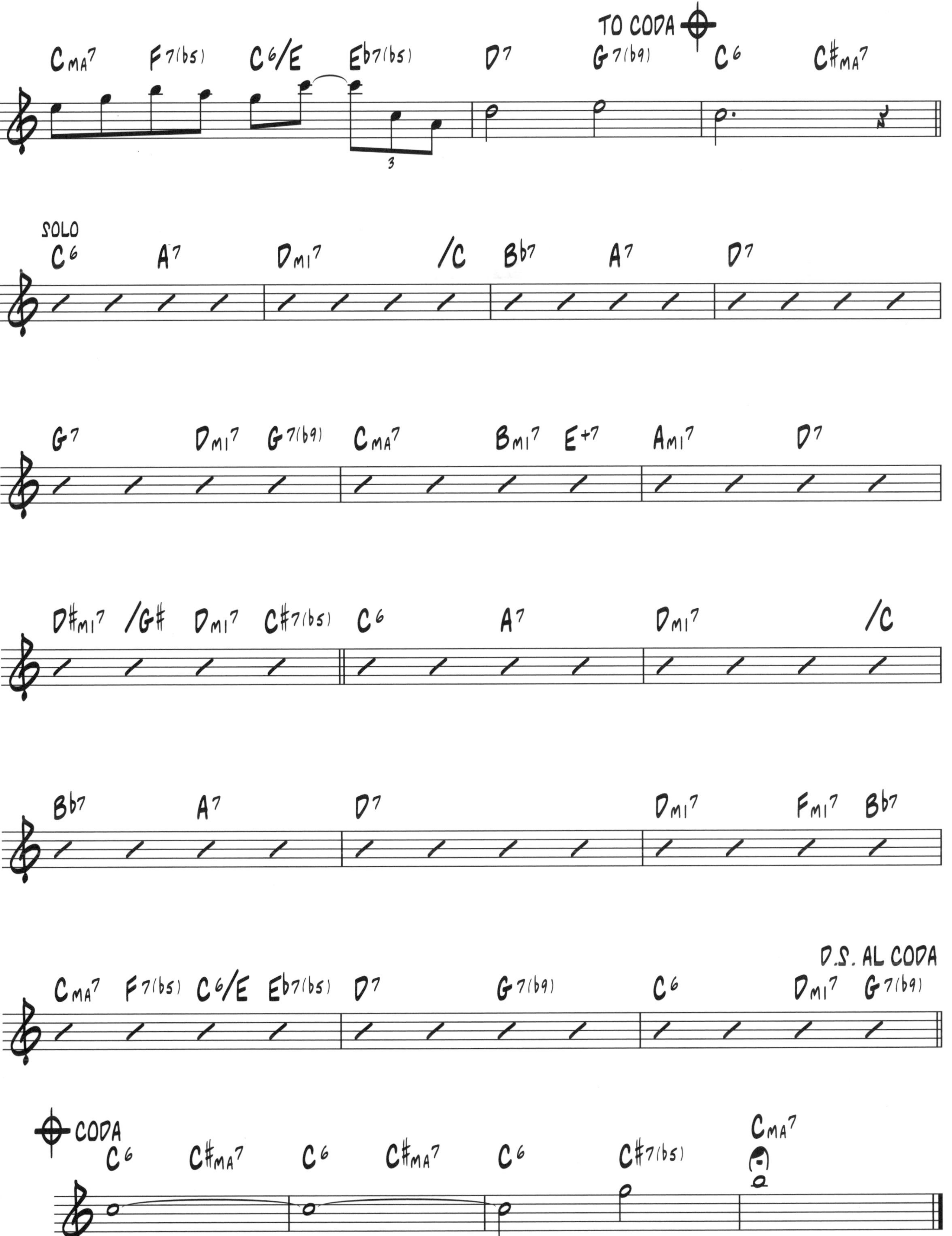
TO CODA
CMA7 F7(b5) C6/E Eb7(b5) D7 G7(b9) C6 C#MA7
SOLO
C6 A7 DMI7 /C Bb7 A7 D7
G7 DMI7 G7(b9) CMA7 BMI7 E+7 AMI7 D7
D#MI7 /G# DMI7 C#7(b5) C6 A7 DMI7 /C
Bb7 A7 D7 DMI7 FMI7 Bb7
D.S. AL CODA
CMA7 F7(b5) C6/E Eb7(b5) D7 G7(b9) C6 DMI7 G7(b9)
CODA
C6 C#MA7 C6 C#MA7 C6 C#7(b5) CMA7
RIT.

CD #2

15: SPLIT TRACK/MELODY
16: FULL STEREO TRACK

ON A SLOW BOAT TO CHINA

BY FRANK LOESSER

Eb VERSION

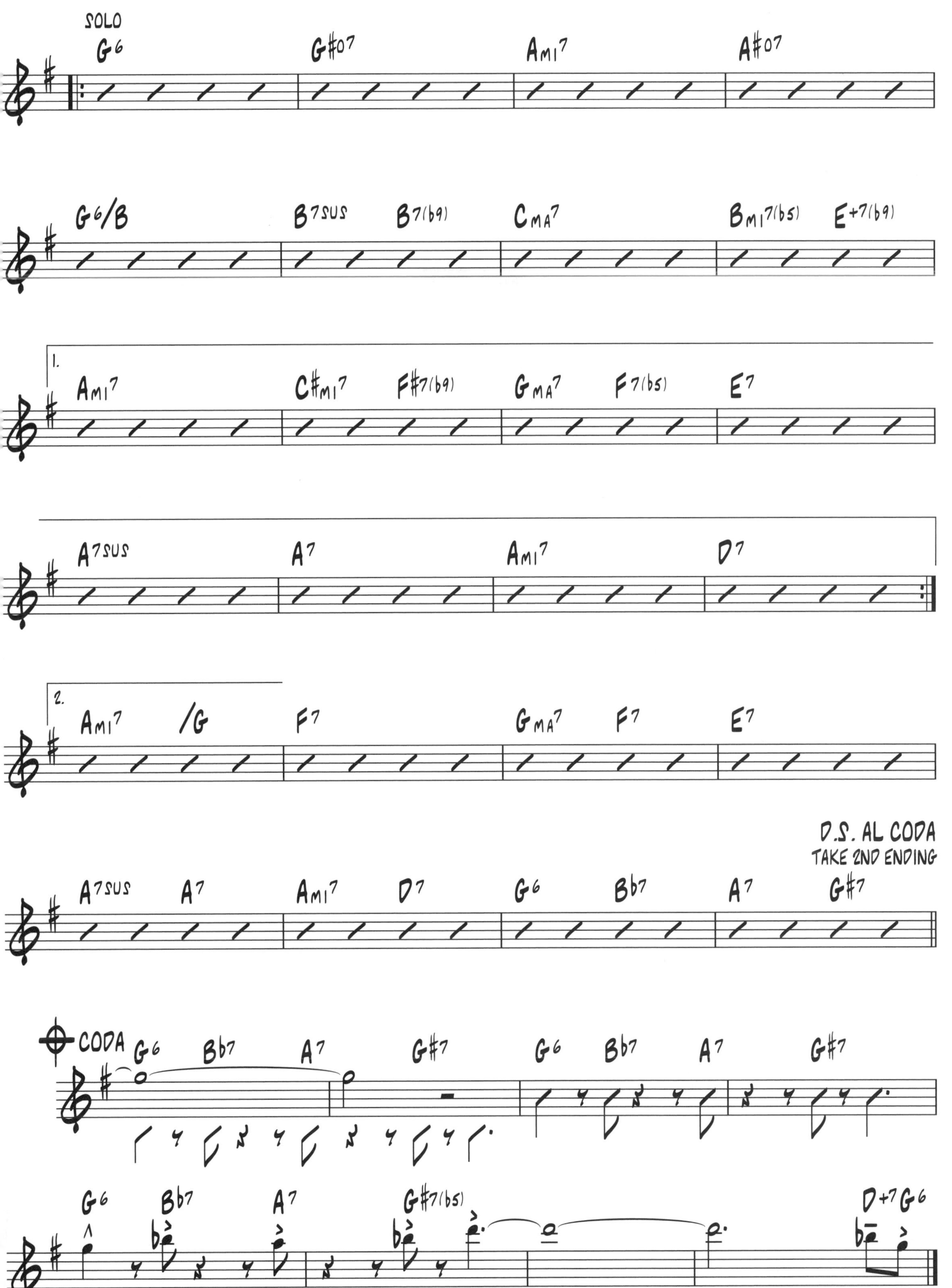
SOLO
G6
G#07
AMI7
A#07
G6/B
B7SUS
B7(b9)
CMA7
BMI7(b5)
E+7(b9)
1.
AMI7
C#MI7
F#7(b9)
GMA7
F7(b5)
E7
A7SUS
A7
AMI7
D7
2.
AMI7
/G
F7
GMA7
F7
E7
D.S. AL CODA
TAKE 2ND ENDING
A7SUS
A7
AMI7
D7
G6
Bb7
A7
G#7
CODA
G6
Bb7
A7
G#7
G6
Bb7
A7
G#7
G6
Bb7
A7
G#7(b5)
D+7
G6

CD #2

17: SPLIT TRACK/MELODY
18: FULL STEREO TRACK

TOO LATE NOW

FROM ROYAL WEDDING

AMA7 /G# F#MI7
BMI7
E7SUS
AMA7 /G# F#MI7
BMI7
E7SUS
AMA7 /G# F#MI7
/E
D#MI7(b5)
D7(b5)
TO CODA
C#MI7 C7 BMI7 E7 A6
BbMA7
SOLO
AMA7 F#MI7 BMI7 E7SUS AMA7 F#MI7
BMI7 E7SUS AMA7 F#MI7
1.
D#MI7(b5) G#+7 C#MI7 C7 BMI7 E7
2.
D#MI7(b5) D7(b5) C#MI7 C7 BMI7 E7 A6 G#MI7 C#+7
F#MI6 G#MI7 C#7 F#MI7 B+7 EMI6
F#MI7 B7(b9) BMI7 E7 AMA7 F#MI7 BMI7 E7SUS AMA7 F#MI7
D.S. AL CODA
BMI7 E7SUS AMA7 F#MI7 D#MI7(b5) D7(b5) C#MI7 C7 BMI7 E7 A6
CODA C#MI7 C7 BMI7 E7 F6 G6 A6
RIT.

CD #2

19 : SPLIT TRACK/MELODY
20 : FULL STEREO TRACK

YOU ARE TOO BEAUTIFUL

FROM HALLELUJAH, I'M A BUM

WORDS BY LORENZ HART
MUSIC BY RICHARD RODGERS

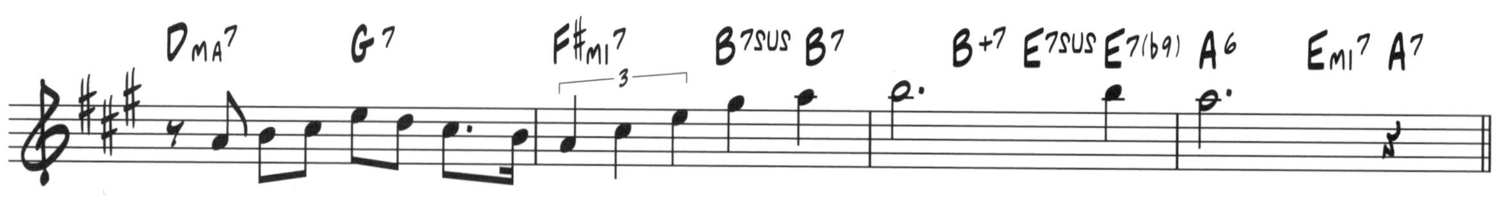

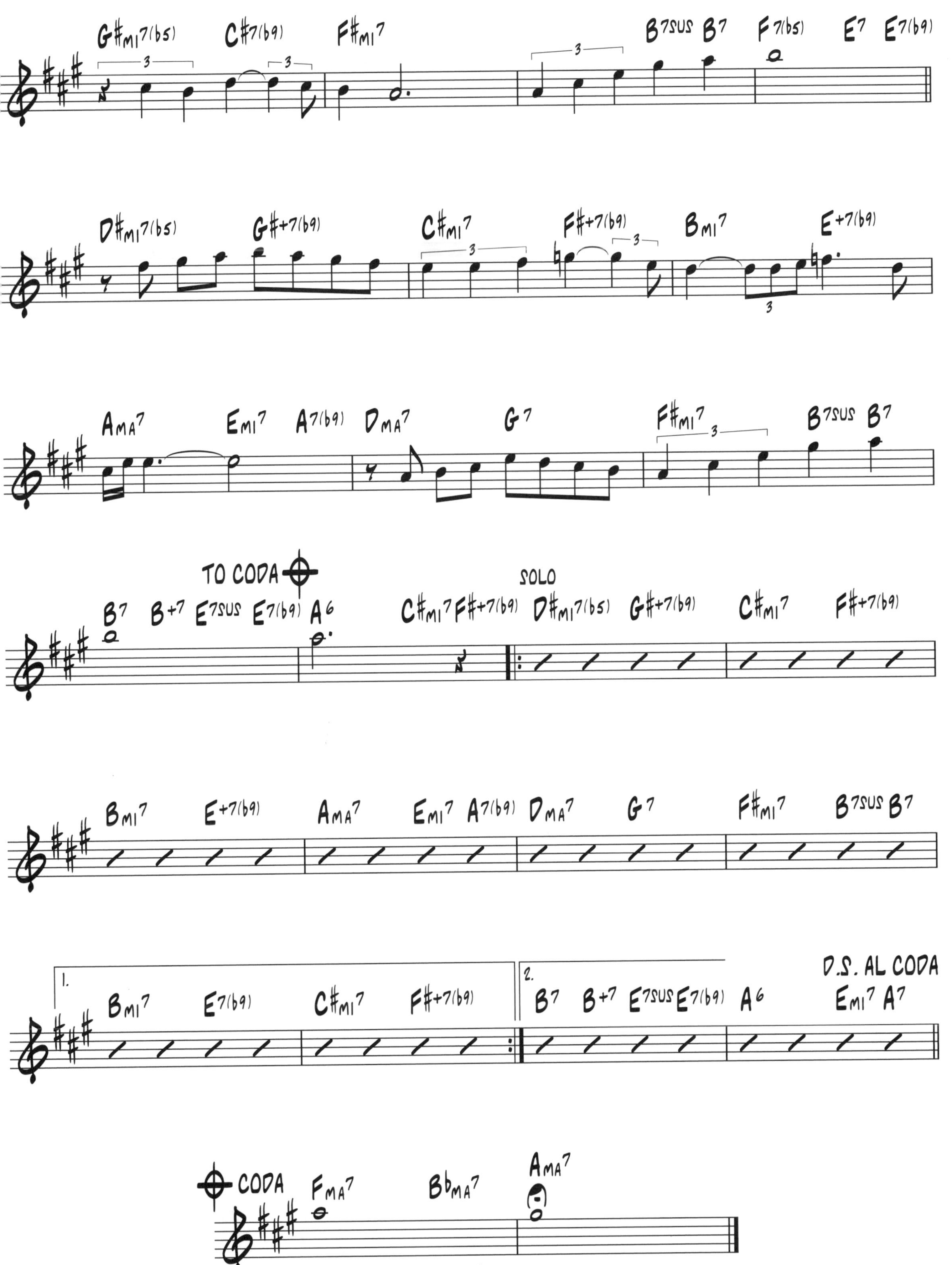
G#MI7(b5) C#7(b9) F#MI7 B7SUS B7 F7(b5) E7 E7(b9)
D#MI7(b5) G#+7(b9) C#MI7 F#+7(b9) BMI7 E+7(b9)
AMA7 EMI7 A7(b9) DMA7 G7 F#MI7 B7SUS B7
TO CODA
SOLO
B7 B+7 E7SUS E7(b9) A6 C#MI7 F#+7(b9) D#MI7(b5) G#+7(b9) C#MI7 F#+7(b9)
BMI7 E+7(b9) AMA7 EMI7 A7(b9) DMA7 G7 F#MI7 B7SUS B7
1.
BMI7 E7(b9) C#MI7 F#+7(b9)
2.
B7 B+7 E7SUS E7(b9) A6
D.S. AL CODA
EMI7 A7
CODA
FMA7 BbMA7 AMA7
RIT.

CD #1

7 : SPLIT TRACK/MELODY
8 : FULL STEREO TRACK

CAN'T HELP LOVIN' DAT MAN

FROM SHOW BOAT

LYRICS BY OSCAR HAMMERSTEIN II
MUSIC BY JEROME KERN

Eb VERSION
SLOW BLUES

Ab7 G7 | Ab7 G7 | E+7(b9) A7 | D+7(b9) G7

RHYTHM

PLAY
mf

CMA7 AMI7 | DMI7 G7 | CMA7 GMI7 F#+7 | FMA7 Bb7

CMA7 Eb7(b5) | 1. Ab7 G+7 G7/F | E+7(b9) A7(#9) | D+7(b9) G7

2. Ab7 G+7 G7(b9) | C6 | GMI7 C+7(b9) | F6 | F#07

C6/G | D7/A | CMA7/G | C07/G | G7SUS

G7SUS G+7(b9) | CMA7 A+7(#9) | DMI7 G7 | CMA7 GMI7 F#+7

TO CODA

FMA7 Bb7 | CMA7 Eb7(b5) | Ab7 G+7 G7(b9) | C6 A7(#9) | D+7(b9) C#7(b9)

SOLO

CMA7 AMI7 | DMI7 G7 | CMA7 GMI7 F#+7 | FMA7 Bb7 | CMA7 Eb7(b5)

Ab7 G+7 G7 | 1. E+7(b9) A7 | D+7(b9) G7 | 2. C6 | GMI7 C+7(b9)

D.S. AL CODA

CODA

Ab7 G+7 G7(b9) FMA7 | Eb7 | DMI7 | C#7(b5) | CMA7(b5)

CD #1
7: SPLIT TRACK/MELODY
8: FULL STEREO TRACK
CAN'T HELP LOVIN' DAT MAN
FROM SHOW BOAT
LYRICS BY OSCAR HAMMERSTEIN II
MUSIC BY JEROME KERN
C VERSION
SLOW BLUES
RHYTHM
PLAY
TO CODA
SOLO
D.S. AL CODA
CODA

CD #1

1: SPLIT TRACK/MELODY
2: FULL STEREO TRACK

C VERSION

ALL THE THINGS YOU ARE

FROM VERY WARM FOR MAY

LYRICS BY OSCAR HAMMERSTEIN II
MUSIC BY JEROME KERN

DbMA7 Gb7 CMI7 B°7
BbMI7 Eb7 TO CODA Ab6 GMI7(b5) C7(b9)
SOLOS (2 CHORUSES)
FMI7 BbMI7 Eb7 AbMA7 DbMA7
DMI7 G7 CMA7 CMI7 FMI7
Bb7 EbMA7 AbMA7 AMI7(b5) D7 GMA7
AMI7 D7 GMA7
F#MI7(b5) B7 EMA7 C+7(b9) FMI7
BbMI7 Eb7 AbMA7 DbMA7 Gb7
D.S. AL CODA
CMI7 B°7 BbMI7 Eb7 Ab6 GMI7(b5) C7(b9)
CODA
N.C. Db7(#9)
1ST X ONLY
1. C7(#9)
2. C7(#9)

CD #1

3: SPLIT TRACK/MELODY

4: FULL STEREO TRACK

ALMOST LIKE BEING IN LOVE

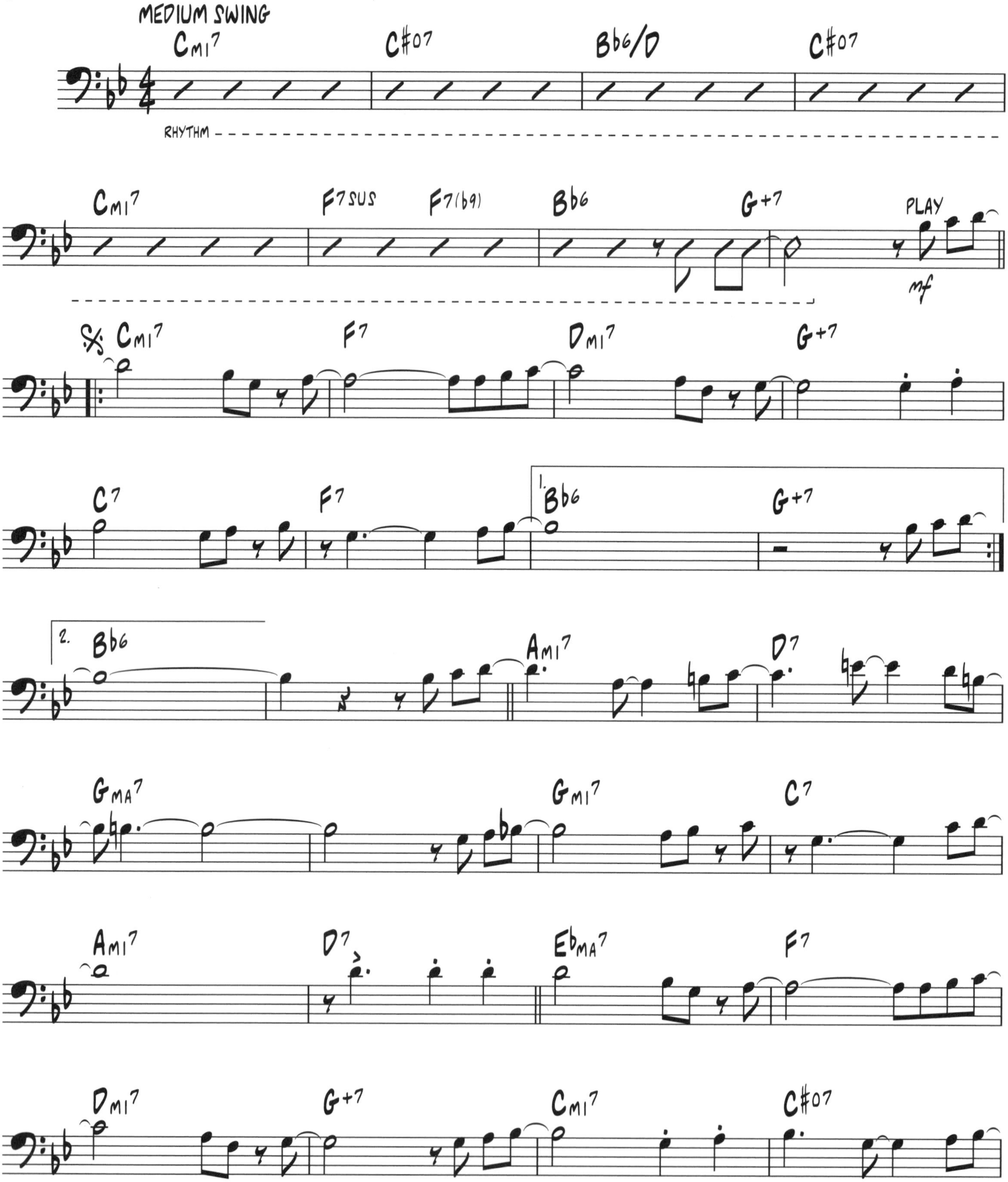

FROM BRIGADOON

LYRICS BY ALAN JAY LERNER
MUSIC BY FREDERICK LOEWE

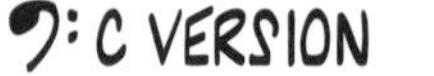

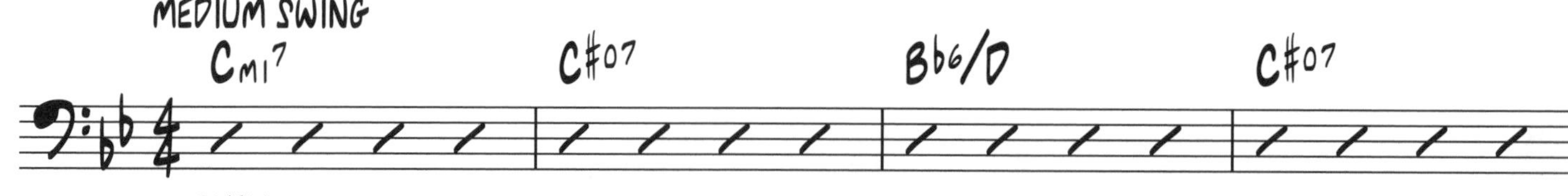

C VERSION

MEDIUM SWING
CMI7
C#O7
Bb6/D
C#O7
RHYTHM
CMI7
F7SUS
F7(b9)
Bb6
G+7
PLAY
mf
CMI7
F7
DMI7
G+7
C7
F7
1. Bb6
G+7
2. Bb6
AMI7
D7
GMA7
GMI7
C7
AMI7
D7
EbMA7
F7
DMI7
G+7
CMI7
C#O7

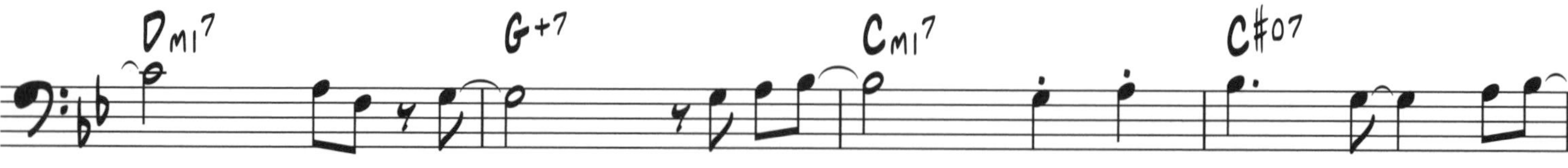

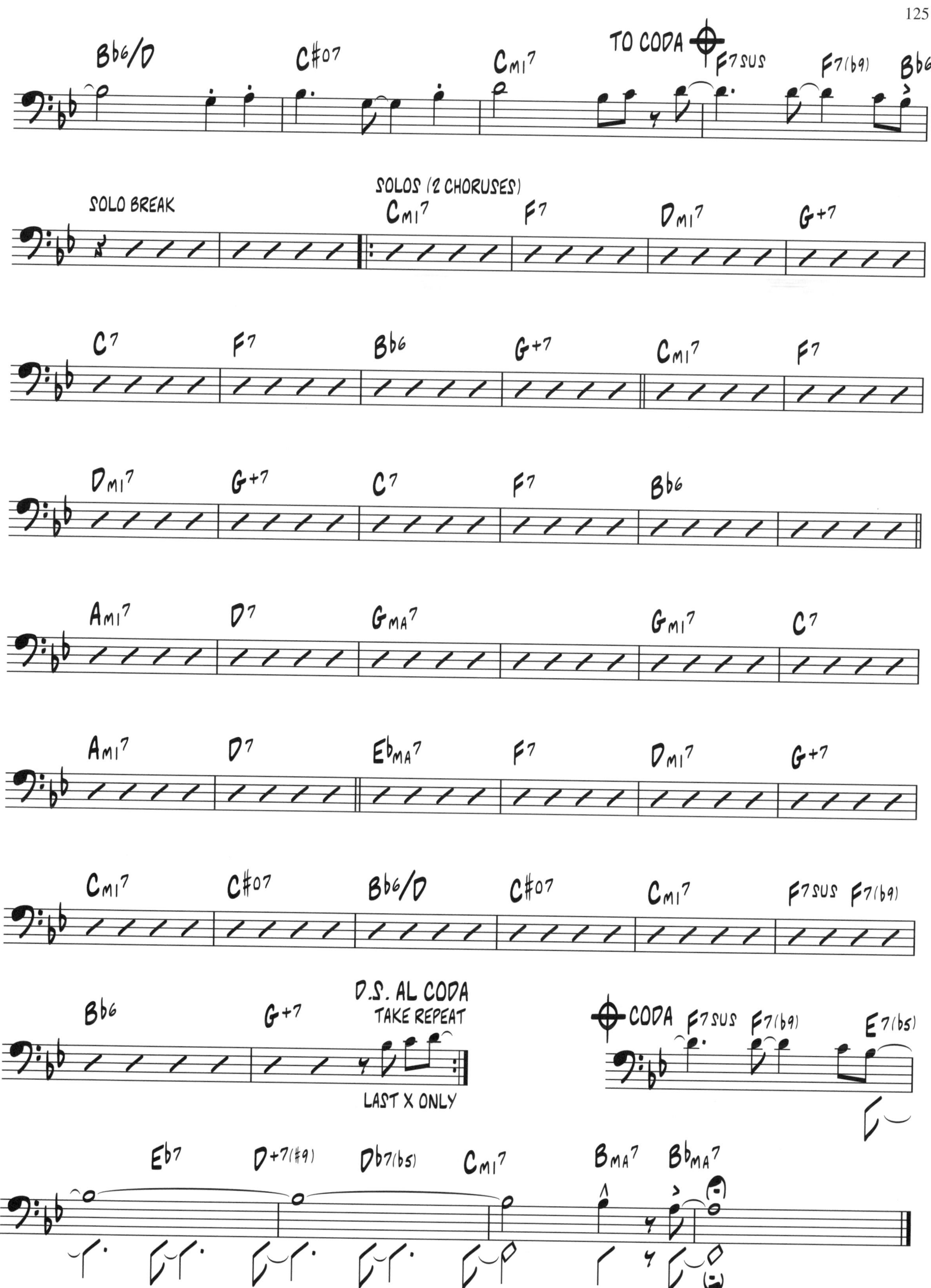
Bb6/D
C#07
CMI7
TO CODA
F7SUS
F7(b9)
Bb6
SOLO BREAK
SOLOS (2 CHORUSES)
CMI7
F7
DMI7
G+7
C7
F7
Bb6
G+7
CMI7
F7
DMI7
G+7
C7
F7
Bb6
AMI7
D7
GMA7
GMI7
C7
AMI7
D7
EbMA7
F7
DMI7
G+7
CMI7
C#07
Bb6/D
C#07
CMI7
F7SUS
F7(b9)
Bb6
G+7
D.S. AL CODA
TAKE REPEAT
LAST X ONLY
CODA
F7SUS
F7(b9)
E7(b5)
Eb7
D+7(#9)
Db7(b5)
CMI7
BMA7
BbMA7

CD #1

5 : SPLIT TRACK/MELODY

6 : FULL STEREO TRACK

BLUE SKIES

FROM BETSY

WORDS AND MUSIC BY
IRVING BERLIN

C VERSION

MEDIUM SALSA

RHYTHM

PLAY

mf

TO CODA

SOLOS (2 FULL CHORUSES)
EMI
B7(b9)/D#
G/D
C#MI7(b5)
G/D
E7(#9)
AMI7
D7
1.
GMA7
C7
F#MI7
B7(b9)
2.
GMA7
F7
F#7
G7
Ab7
G7
F7
G7
C7
D7
G7
Ab7
G7
F7
G7
F#7
B7
EMI
B7(b9)/D#
G/D
C#MI7(b5)
D.S. AL CODA
TAKE REPEAT
G/D
E7(#9)
AMI7
D7
GMA7
AMI7
D7(#9)
EbMI7
CODA
G/D
E7(#9)
AMI7
D7
GMA7
E7(#9)
AMI7
D7(b9)
GMA7
E7(#9)
AMI7
D7
GMA7
Bb7
Eb7
Ab7
3
GMA7
E7(#9)
AMI7
D7
GMA7
F7
F#7
G6

CD #1

9: SPLIT TRACK/MELODY

10: FULL STEREO TRACK

COME RAIN OR COME SHINE

FROM ST. LOUIS WOMAN

WORDS BY JOHNNY MERCER
MUSIC BY HAROLD ARLEN

TO CODA
DMI7 B+7(#9) Bb7(b5) A7(b9) D7(#9) G7 G+7 C7SUS C7(b9)
SOLO
FMA7 EMI7 A+7 DMI7
G7SUS G+7 C7SUS C7(b9) FMA7 Db7 CMI7 B7(b5)
BbMI7 FMI6 B7(b5) BbMI7 Ab7 GMI7(b5) C7(b9)
BMI7(b5) E7(b9) AMI7(b5) D7(b9) AMI7(b5) D+7(b9) G7 C7SUS C7(b9)
FMA7 EMI7 A+7 DMI7 Eb7(b5) DMI7
AbMI7 Db7 F#MI7 B+7 EMI7 A+7 EMI7 Eb7(b5)
D7SUS EMI7 Fo7 D7/F# G7SUS AMI7 BbMA7 A+7 A7(b9)
DMI7 B+7(#9) Bb7(b5) A7(b9) D7(#9) G7 G+7 C7SUS C7(b9)
D.S. AL CODA
CODA D7(#9) G7 A+7 DMI7
4X'S
1ST X ONLY
RIT. LAST TIME

CD #1

11: SPLIT TRACK/MELODY
12: FULL STEREO TRACK

DESAFINADO

ORIGINAL TEXT BY NEWTON MENDONÇA
MUSIC BY ANTONIO CARLOS JOBIM

𝄢: C VERSION

D7(b9) G7SUS G+7 C7SUS C7(b9) FMA7
G7(b5) GMI7 C7 AMI7(b5)
D+7(#9) D7(b9) GMI7 Eb7 FMA7 Abo
G7SUS G7 G7SUS G7 Eb7SUS Eb7 Eb7SUS Eb7 G7SUS G7
TO CODA
SOLO
GMI7 C7 FMA7 Gb7(b5) FMA7 G7(b5)
GMI7 C7 AMI7(b5) D7(b9) GMI7 EMI7(b5) A7(b9) 1. DMA7
D7(b9) G7 G7(b9) GbMA7 Gb7(b5) 2. DMI7 E7
AMA7 Ab+7 G7 Gb7 AMA7 Bbo BMI7
E7 AMA7 F#MI7 BMI7 E7 CMA7
D.S. AL CODA
C#o DMI7 G7 GMI7 D7(b9) GMI7 C7
CODA
FMA7 Gb7(b5) FMA7 Gb7(b5)
3
FMA7 Gb7(b5) FMA7

CD #1

13: SPLIT TRACK/MELODY

14: FULL STEREO TRACK

DON'T GET AROUND MUCH ANYMORE

FROM SOPHISTICATED LADY

C VERSION

WORDS AND MUSIC BY DUKE ELLINGTON
AND BOB RUSSELL

SOLO
CMA7
A7
D7
G7
1.
CMA7
DMI7
G7
2.
CMA7
Ab7
GMI7
C7
FMA7
F#o7
CMA7/G
C7
FMA7
F#o7
B7(b9)
EMI7
Ebo7
DMI7
G7
CMA7
A7
D7
G7
CMA7
N.C./G
D.S. AL CODA
TAKE REPEAT
CODA
CMA7
G7
RHYTHM
CMA7
G7
RHYTHM
CMA7
Ab7
G7
C6
RHYTHM

CD #1

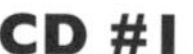

15: SPLIT TRACK/MELODY
16: FULL STEREO TRACK

FOR ALL WE KNOW

FROM THE MOTION PICTURE LOVERS AND OTHER STRANGERS

WORDS BY ROBB WILSON AND ARTHUR JAMES
MUSIC BY FRED KARLIN

𝄢: C VERSION

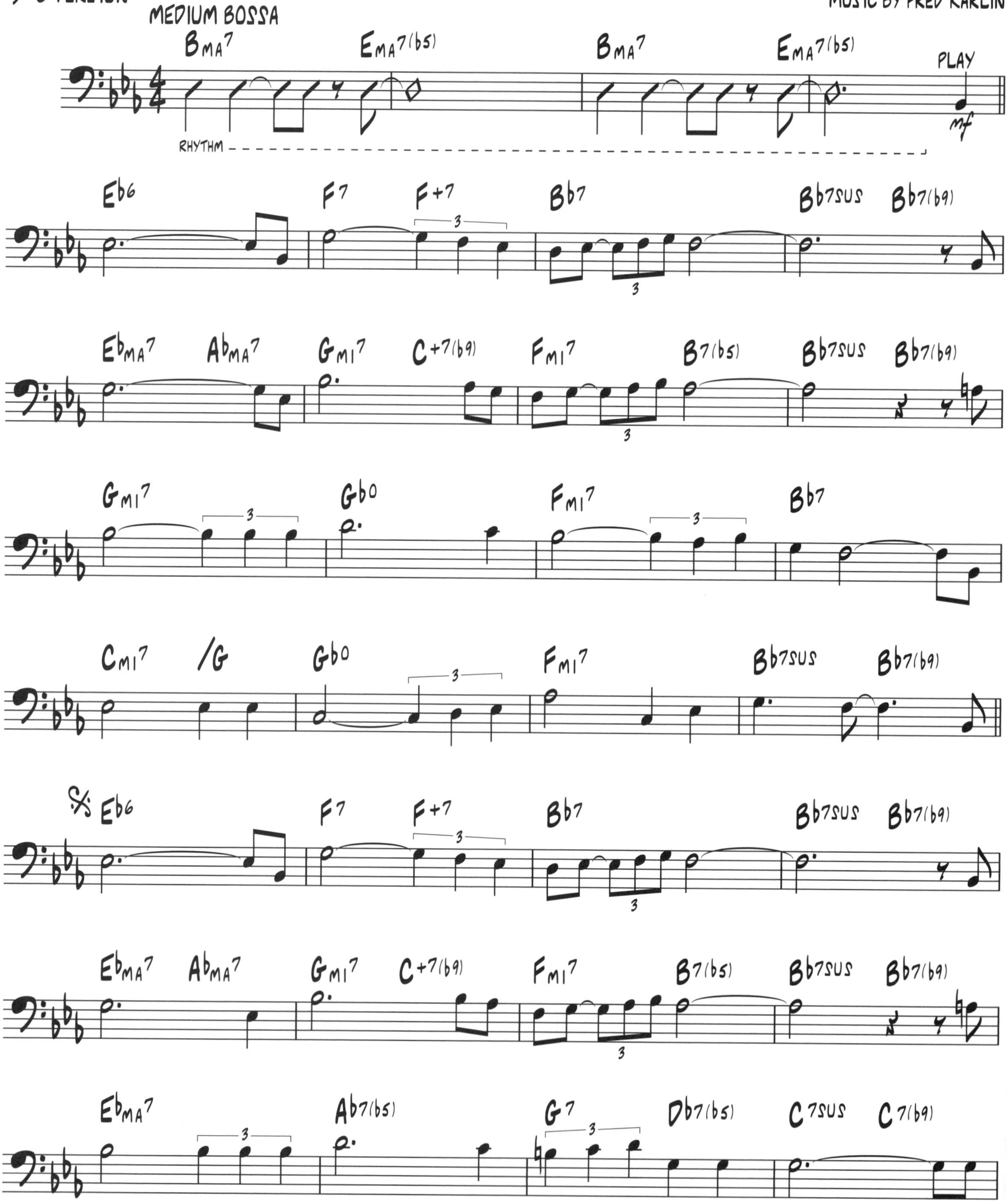
MEDIUM BOSSA
BMA7 EMA7(b5) BMA7 EMA7(b5)
PLAY
RHYTHM
mf
Eb6 F7 F+7 Bb7 Bb7SUS Bb7(b9)
EbMA7 AbMA7 GMI7 C+7(b9) FMI7 B7(b5) Bb7SUS Bb7(b9)
GMI7 Gbo FMI7 Bb7
CMI7 /G Gbo FMI7 Bb7SUS Bb7(b9)
Eb6 F7 F+7 Bb7 Bb7SUS Bb7(b9)
EbMA7 AbMA7 GMI7 C+7(b9) FMI7 B7(b5) Bb7SUS Bb7(b9)
EbMA7 Ab7(b5) G7 Db7(b5) C7SUS C7(b9)

TO CODA
FMI7 B7(b5) Bb7SUS Bb7(b9) BMA7 EMA7(b5)
SOLO
Eb6 F7 F+7 Bb7 Bb7SUS Bb7(b9) EbMA7 AbMA7
GMI7 C+7(b9) FMI7 B7(b5) Bb7SUS Bb7(b9) GMI7 Gb0
FMI7 Bb7 CMI7 /G Gb0 FMI7
Bb7SUS Bb7(b9) Eb6 F7 F+7 Bb7 Bb7SUS Bb7(b9)
EbMA7 AbMA7 GMI7 C+7(b9) FMI7 B7(b5) Bb7SUS Bb7(b9)
EbMA7 Ab7(b5) G7 Db7(b5) C7SUS C7(b9)
FMI7 B7(b5) Bb7SUS Bb7(b9) BMA7 EMA7(b5) D.S. AL CODA
CODA
BMA7 EMA7(b5) BMA7 EMA7(b5) EbMA7(b5)
RIT.
RHYTHM

CD #1

17: SPLIT TRACK/MELODY

18: FULL STEREO TRACK

I GOTTA RIGHT TO SING THE BLUES

WORDS BY TED KOEHLER
MUSIC BY HAROLD ARLEN

C VERSION

SLOW BLUES

Bb7 Eb7 Bb7 A7 Ab7 G7 PLAY C7SUS C7

RHYTHM mf

F7 F+7

Bb7SUS Bb7 Fmi7 Bb7 Dmi7(b5)

G+7 G7 C7SUS C7

F7 Bb7 Bb7SUS

Bbo7 Bb7 Ebmi6/Bb Bbo7 Bb7 A+7 Ab7 G7

C7SUS C7 F7 F+7

Bb7SUS Bb7 Fmi7 Bb7

DMI7(b5)
G+7
G7
C7
Ab7(b5)
GMI7
C7
TO CODA
CMI7
Gb7
F7
Bb7
Eb7
Bb7
A7
Ab7
G7
SOLO
C7
F7
Bb7
DMI7(b5)
G7
C7
F7
Bb7
Bb7SUS
Bbo7
Bb7
EbMI6/Bb
Bbo7
Bb7
A+7
Ab7
G7
D.S. AL CODA
CODA
Bb7
B7(b5)
Bb7(b5)
RIT.

CD #1
19: SPLIT TRACK/MELODY
20: FULL STEREO TRACK

I WISH I DIDN'T LOVE YOU SO

FROM THE PARAMOUNT PICTURE THE PERILS OF PAULINE

WORDS AND MUSIC BY
FRANK LOESSER

C VERSION

SOLO
Eb6 AbMA7 GMI7 C7 FMI7 Bb7(b9) EbMA7 BbMI7 Eb7 AbMA7 Db7
GMI7 C7 FMI7 Bb7SUS G+7 Gb7 FMI7 E7(b5)
Eb6 AbMA7 GMI7 C7 FMI7 Bb7(b9) EbMA7 A+7(b9) AbMA7 Db7
GMI7 C7 FMI7 Bb7SUS Eb6 AbMA7 Eb6
GMI7(b5) C7(b9) GMI7(b5) C7(b9) FMI7
G+7(b9) Db7(b5) C7 C7(b5) F7SUS F7 FMI7 E7(b5)
Eb6 AbMA7 GMI7 C7 FMI7 Bb7(b9) EbMA7 A+7(b9) AbMA7 Db7
GMI7 C7 FMI7 Bb7SUS Eb6 AbMA7 Eb6
D.S. AL CODA
CODA
AbMA7 Db7 Gb7 Cb7 FMI7 E7(b5) EbMA7

CD #2

1 : SPLIT TRACK/MELODY
2 : FULL STEREO TRACK

I'LL TAKE ROMANCE

LYRICS BY OSCAR HAMMERSTEIN II
MUSIC BY BEN OAKLAND

A+7(b9) D7(b9) Gmi7 C7(b9) F6
SOLO BREAK
SOLOS (2 CHORUSES)
4 FEEL
F6 Dmi7 Gmi7 C7 /Bb Ami7 Ab7 Db6 Gbma7 A+7(b9) D7(b9)
Gmi7 C7(b9) F6 Ab7 Db6 C7 F6 Dmi7 Gmi7 C7 /Bb
Ami7 Ab7 Db6 Gbma7 A+7(b9) D7(b9) Gmi7 C7(b9) F6 C7sus F6
Ebmi7 Ab7 Dbma7 Bbmi7 Ebmi7 Ab7 Dbma7 C#mi7 F#7 Bma7 Ema7
A+7 Ab7 Dbma7 C7 C#o Dmi7 /C Bmi7(b5) Bbmi6 Ami7 Ab7
D.S. AL CODA
Db6 Gbma7 A+7(b9) D7(b9) Gmi7 C7(b9) F6 Ab7 Db6 C7
CODA
A+7(b9) D7(b9) Gmi7 C7(b9) F6 Ab7 Db6 C7sus
F6 Ab7 Db6 C7sus Gbma7 Fma7

CD #2

IN THE WEE SMALL HOURS OF THE MORNING

C VERSION

WORDS BY BOB HILLIARD
MUSIC BY DAVID MANN

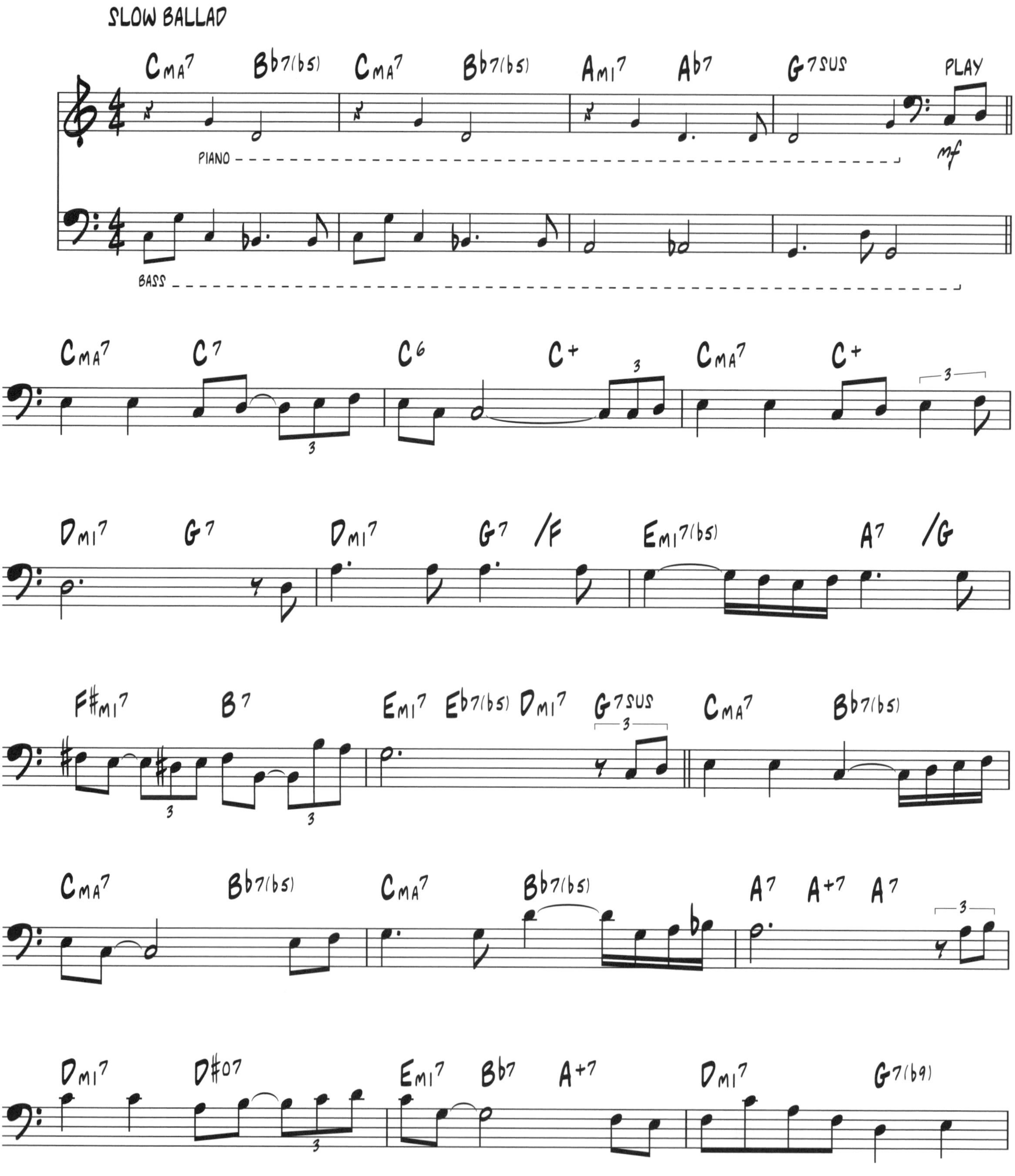

SLOW BALLAD

CMA7 Bb7(b5) CMA7 Bb7(b5) AMI7 Ab7 G7SUS PLAY

PIANO

mf

BASS

CMA7 C7 C6 C+ CMA7 C+

DMI7 G7 DMI7 G7 /F EMI7(b5) A7 /G

F#MI7 B7 EMI7 Eb7(b5) DMI7 G7SUS CMA7 Bb7(b5)

CMA7 Bb7(b5) CMA7 Bb7(b5) A7 A+7 A7

DMI7 D#o7 EMI7 Bb7 A+7 DMI7 G7(b9)

C6 Db7(b5)
SOLO
CMA7 C7 C6 C+
CMA7 C+ DMI7 G7 DMI7 G7 /F
EMI7(b5) A7 /G F#MI7 B7 EMI7 Eb7(b5) DMI7 G7SUS
CMA7 Bb7(b5) CMA7 Bb7(b5) CMA7 Bb7(b5)
A7 A+7 A7 DMI7 D#O7 EMI7 Bb7 A+7
3
3
DMI7 G7 /F EMI7 A+7 DMI7 G7(b9)
FMA7 Eb6 DMI7 DbMA7 CMA7
RIT.

CD #2

5 : SPLIT TRACK/MELODY

6 : FULL STEREO TRACK

JUST IN TIME

FROM BELLS ARE RINGING

WORDS BY BETTY COMDEN AND ADOLPH GREEN
MUSIC BY JULE STYNE

C VERSION

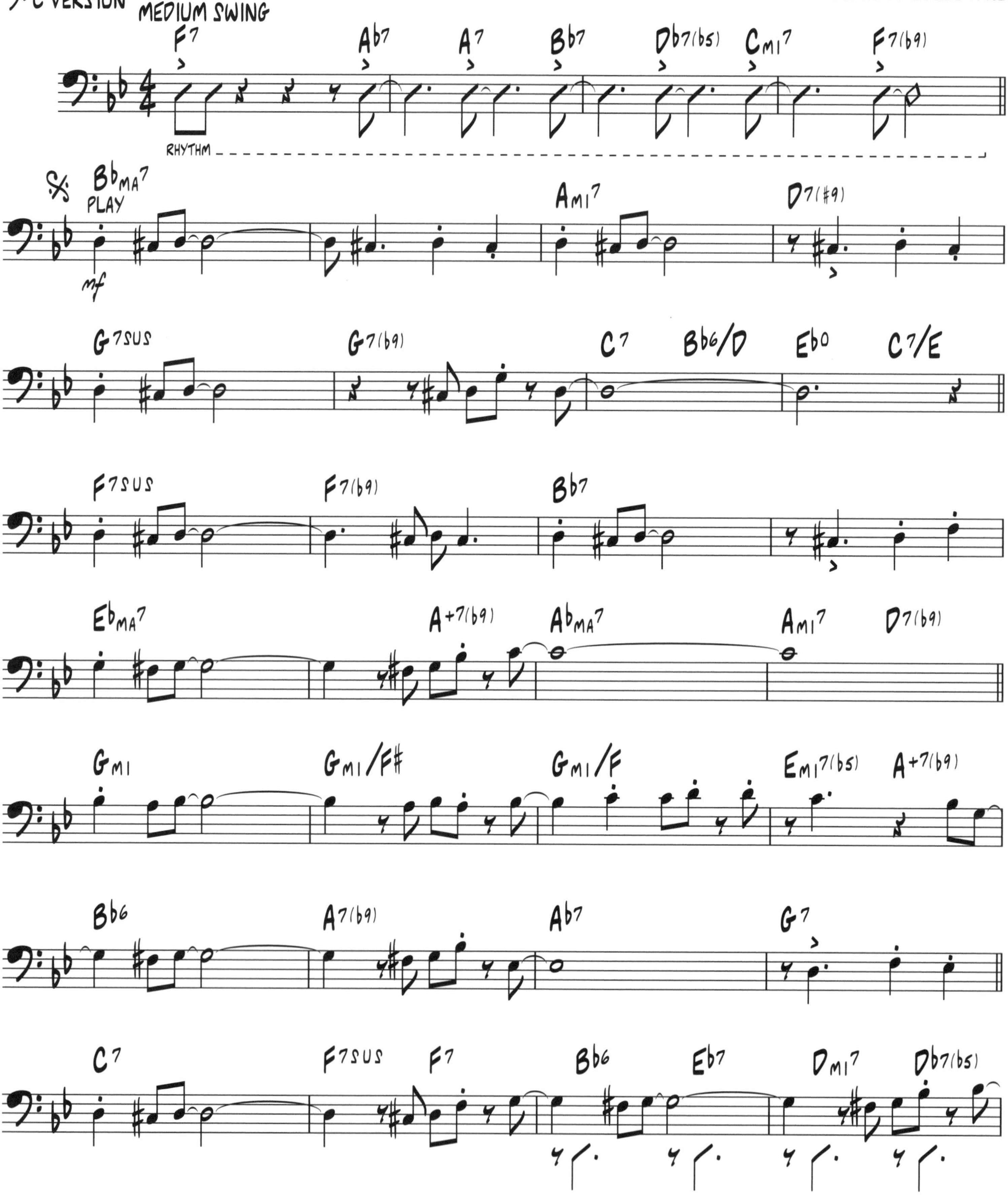

MEDIUM SWING
F7 Ab7 A7 Bb7 Db7(b5) Cmi7 F7(b9)
RHYTHM
BbMA7
PLAY
mf
Ami7 D7(#9)
G7SUS G7(b9) C7 Bb6/D Eb° C7/E
F7SUS F7(b9) Bb7
EbMA7 A+7(b9) AbMA7 Ami7 D7(b9)
Gmi Gmi/F# Gmi/F Emi7(b5) A+7(b9)
Bb6 A7(b9) Ab7 G7
C7 F7SUS F7 Bb6 Eb7 Dmi7 Db7(b5)

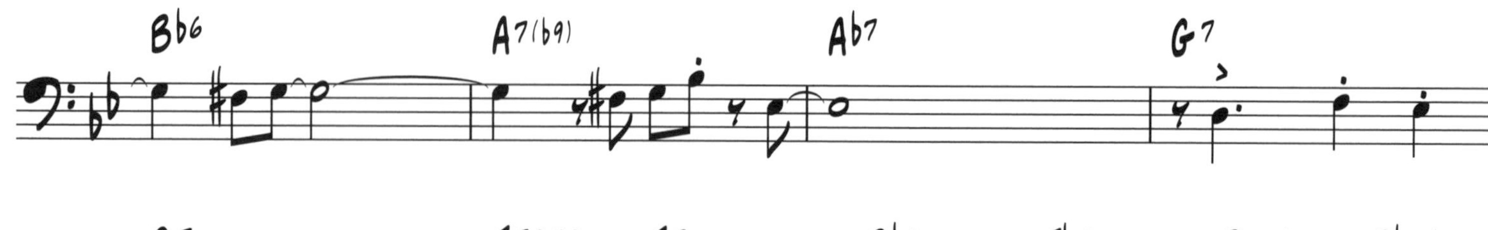

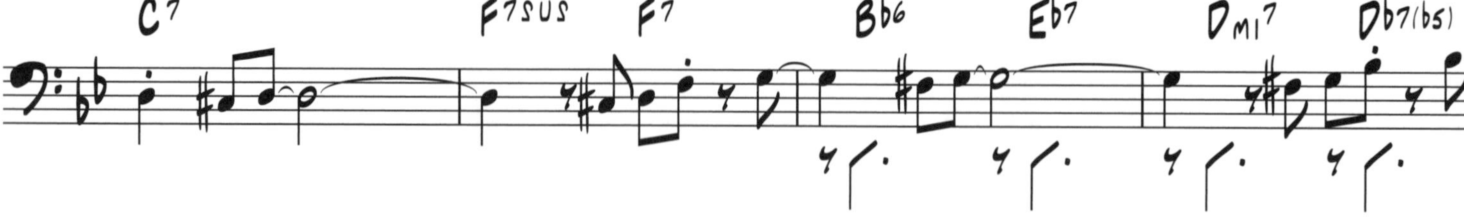

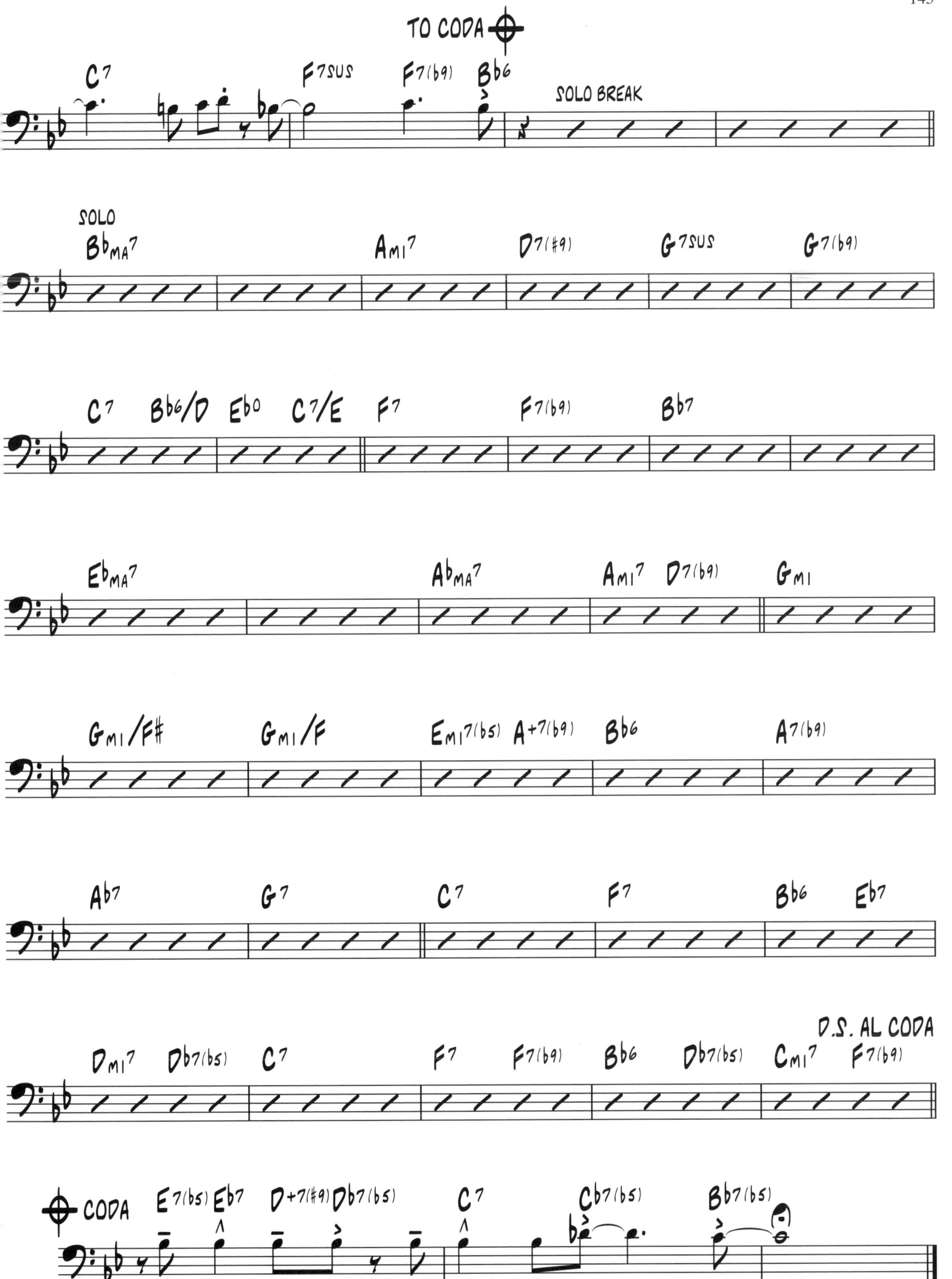
TO CODA
C7
F7SUS
F7(b9)
Bb6
SOLO BREAK
SOLO
BbMA7
AMI7
D7(#9)
G7SUS
G7(b9)
C7
Bb6/D
Eb0
C7/E
F7
F7(b9)
Bb7
EbMA7
AbMA7
AMI7
D7(b9)
GMI
GMI/F#
GMI/F
EMI7(b5)
A+7(b9)
Bb6
A7(b9)
Ab7
G7
C7
F7
Bb6
Eb7
D.S. AL CODA
DMI7
Db7(b5)
C7
F7
F7(b9)
Bb6
Db7(b5)
CMI7
F7(b9)
CODA
E7(b5)
Eb7
D+7(#9)
Db7(b5)
C7
Cb7(b5)
Bb7(b5)

CD #2

7: SPLIT TRACK/MELODY
8: FULL STEREO TRACK

LIKE SOMEONE IN LOVE

WORDS BY JOHNNY BURKE
MUSIC BY JIMMY VAN HEUSEN

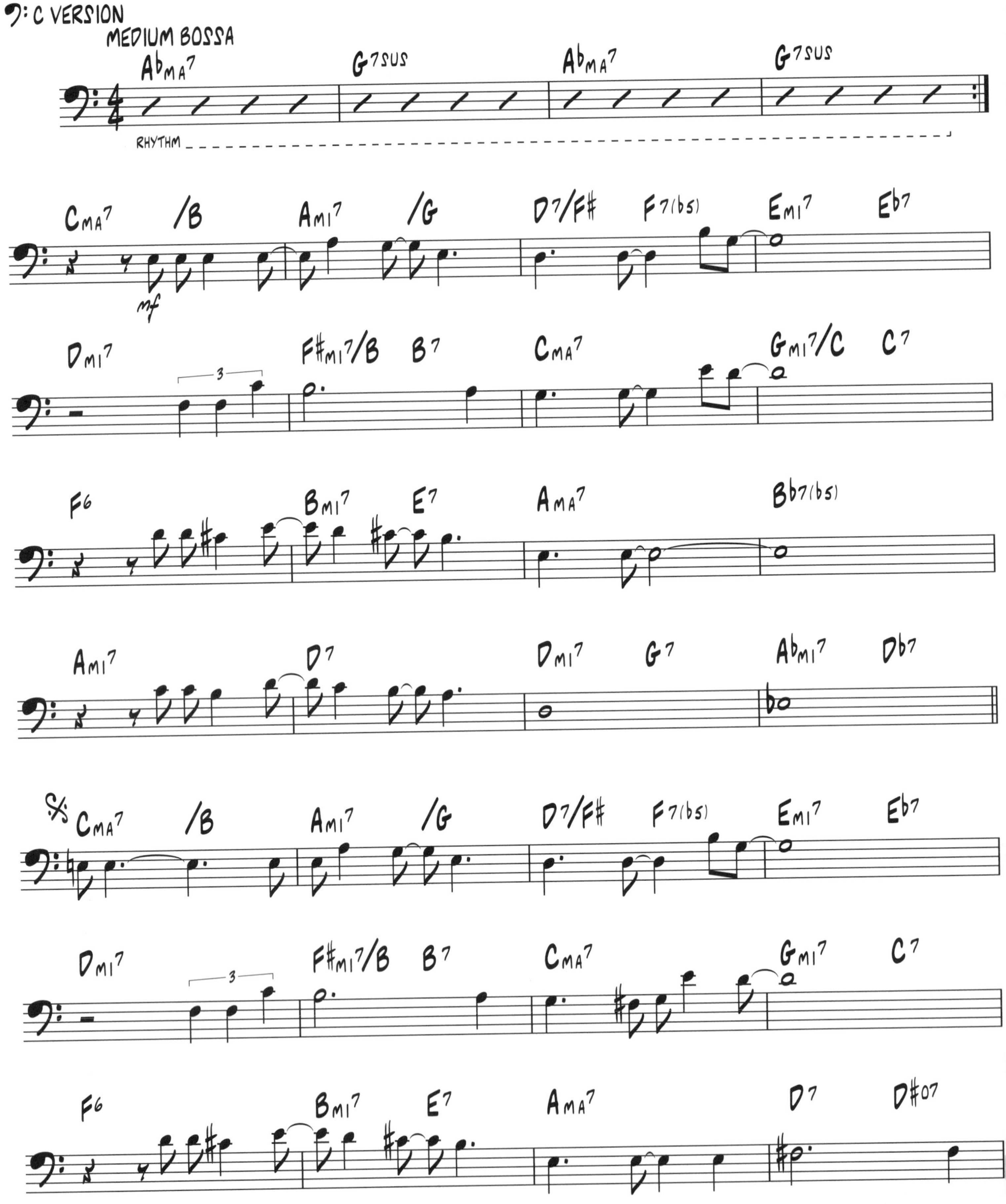
C VERSION
MEDIUM BOSSA
Abma7 G7sus Abma7 G7sus
RHYTHM
Cma7 /B Ami7 /G D7/F# F7(b5) Emi7 Eb7
mf
Dmi7 F#mi7/B B7 Cma7 Gmi7/C C7
3
F6 Bmi7 E7 Ama7 Bb7(b5)
Ami7 D7 Dmi7 G7 Abmi7 Db7
Cma7 /B Ami7 /G D7/F# F7(b5) Emi7 Eb7
Dmi7 F#mi7/B B7 Cma7 Gmi7 C7
3
F6 Bmi7 E7 Ama7 D7 D#o7

TO CODA

EMI7 A7 DMI7 G7(b9) C6 AbMA7 G7SUS

SOLO

CMA7 /B AMI7 /G D7/F# F7(b5) EMI7 Eb7 DMI7

F#MI7 B7 CMA7 GMI7/C C7 F6 BMI7 E7

AMA7 Bb7(b5) AMI7 D7 DMI7 G7 AbMI7 Db7

CMA7 /B AMI7 /G D7/F# F7(b5) EMI7 Eb7 DMI7 F#MI7 B7

CMA7 GMI7 C7 F6 BMI7 E7 AMA7

D.S. AL CODA

D7 D#07 EMI7 A7 DMI7 G7(b9) C6 AbMA7 G7SUS

CODA

C6 AbMA7 G7SUS C6 AbMA7 G7SUS

C6 AbMA7 G7SUS CMA7

CD #2

9: SPLIT TRACK/MELODY
10: FULL STEREO TRACK

LOLLIPOPS AND ROSES

WORDS AND MUSIC BY
TONY VELONA

C VERSION

DMI7 G7(b9) GMI7 C7SUS Ab7 GMI7
C7 /Bb AMI7 DMI7 D#07 EMI7(b5)
AMI7 D+7(#9) GMI7 C7(b9) FMA7
TO CODA
Eb7 /Db F6/C C7SUS F6/C A+7 Ab7
SOLO
GMI7 C7 /Bb AMI7 DMI7 D#07 EMI7(b5)
AMI7 D+7(#9) GMI7 C7(b9) FMA7 Eb7 /Db
F6/C C7SUS F6/C
1. AMI7 Ab7
2. D.S. AL CODA AMI7 D7(#9)
CODA
F6/C C7SUS F6/C D7(#9)
GMI7 C7SUS GMI7 GbMA7 FMA7

CD #2

11 : SPLIT TRACK/MELODY
12 : FULL STEREO TRACK

LOVE IS JUST AROUND THE CORNER

FROM THE PARAMOUNT PICTURE HERE IS MY HEART

WORDS AND MUSIC BY LEO ROBIN
AND LEWIS E. GENSLER

𝄢: C VERSION

SOLOS (2 CHORUSES)
G7/B C7/Bb F6/A D+7(b9) G7/B C7/Bb F6/A D+7(b9)
G7/B C7/Bb F6/A Ab7 G7 C7(b9) F6 Ab7/C
G7/B C7/Bb F6/A D+7(b9) G7/B C7/Bb F6/A D+7(b9)
G7/B C7/Bb F6/A Ab7 G7 C7(b9) F6 Emi7 A+7(b9)
Dmi7 B7(#9) Emi7 A+7(b9) Dmi7 G7 Emi7 A7
Dmi7 G7 Gmi7 C7(b9) G7/B C7/Bb F6/A D+7(b9) G7/B C7/Bb
F6/A D+7(b9) G7/B C7/Bb F6/A Ab7 G7 C7(b9) F6 D.S. AL CODA
CODA
G7 C7SUS C7(b9) F6 Ab7 G7 C7SUS C7(b9) F6 D+7(#9)
G7 C7SUS C7(b9) F6 Bb7 A7 Ab7 G7(b5) Gb7(b5) FMA7(b5)

CD #2

13: SPLIT TRACK/MELODY

14: FULL STEREO TRACK

C VERSION

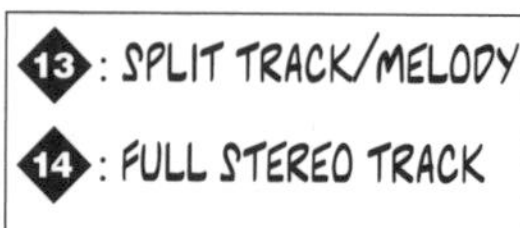

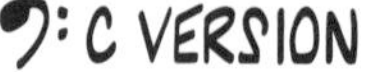

MY IDEAL

FROM THE PARAMOUNT PICTURE PLAYBOY OF PARIS

WORDS BY LEO ROBIN

MUSIC BY RICHARD A. WHITING AND NEWELL CHASE

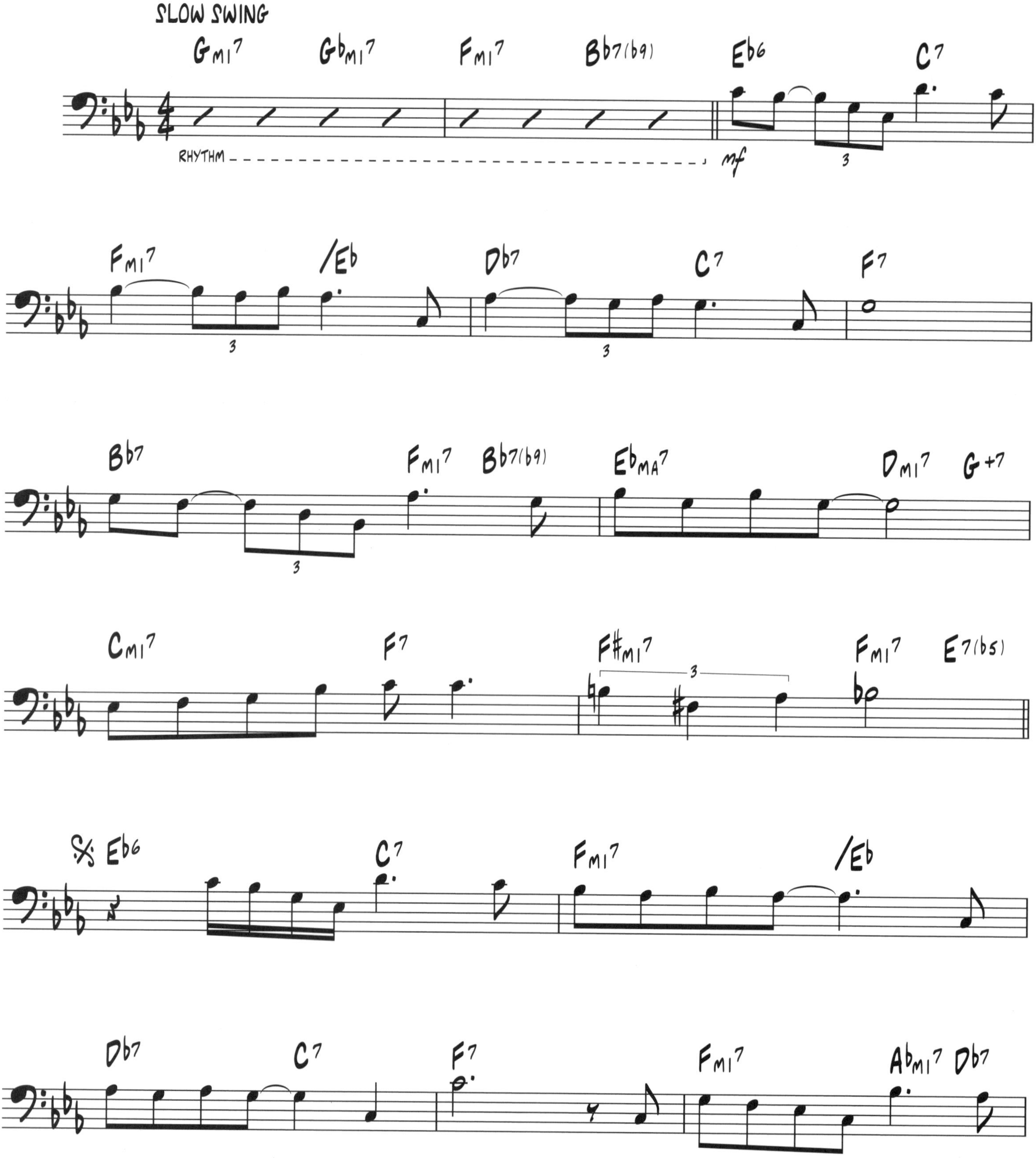
SLOW SWING
Gmi7 Gbmi7 Fmi7 Bb7(b9) Eb6 C7
RHYTHM
mf
Fmi7 /Eb Db7 C7 F7
Bb7 Fmi7 Bb7(b9) Ebma7 Dmi7 G+7
Cmi7 F7 F#mi7 Fmi7 E7(b5)
Eb6 C7 Fmi7 /Eb
Db7 C7 F7 Fmi7 Abmi7 Db7

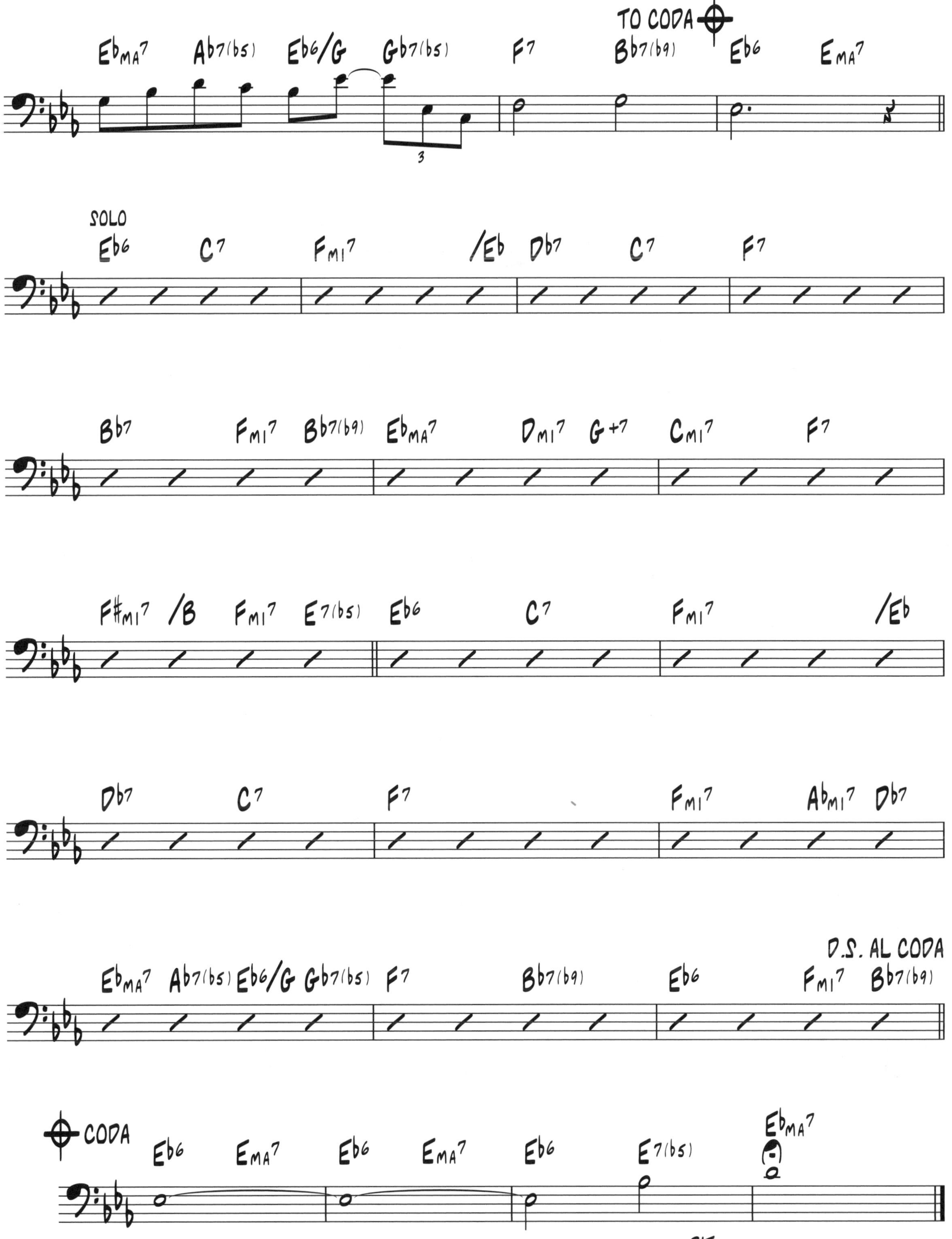
TO CODA
Eb MA7 Ab7(b5) Eb6/G Gb7(b5) F7 Bb7(b9) Eb6 E MA7
3
SOLO
Eb6 C7 F MI7 /Eb Db7 C7 F7
Bb7 F MI7 Bb7(b9) Eb MA7 D MI7 G+7 C MI7 F7
F# MI7 /B F MI7 E7(b5) Eb6 C7 F MI7 /Eb
Db7 C7 F7 F MI7 Ab MI7 Db7
D.S. AL CODA
Eb MA7 Ab7(b5) Eb6/G Gb7(b5) F7 Bb7(b9) Eb6 F MI7 Bb7(b9)
CODA
Eb6 E MA7 Eb6 E MA7 Eb6 E7(b5) Eb MA7
RIT.

CD #2

15: SPLIT TRACK/MELODY
16: FULL STEREO TRACK

C VERSION

ON A SLOW BOAT TO CHINA

BY FRANK LOESSER

SOLO
Bb6 B07 Cmi7 C#07
Bb6/D D7SUS D7(b9) EbmA7 Dmi7(b5) G+7(b9)
1.
Cmi7 Emi7 A7(b9) BbmA7 Ab7(b5) G7
C7SUS C7 Cmi7 F7
2.
Cmi7 /Bb Ab7 BbmA7 Ab7 G7
D.S. AL CODA
TAKE 2ND ENDING
C7SUS C7 Cmi7 F7 Bb6 Db7 C7 B7
CODA Bb6 Db7 C7 B7 Bb6 Db7 C7 B7
Bb6 Db7 C7 B7(b5) F+7 Bb6

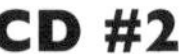

CD #2

17: SPLIT TRACK/MELODY
18: FULL STEREO TRACK

TOO LATE NOW

FROM ROYAL WEDDING

WORDS BY ALAN JAY LERNER
MUSIC BY BURTON LANE

C VERSION

SLOW SWING

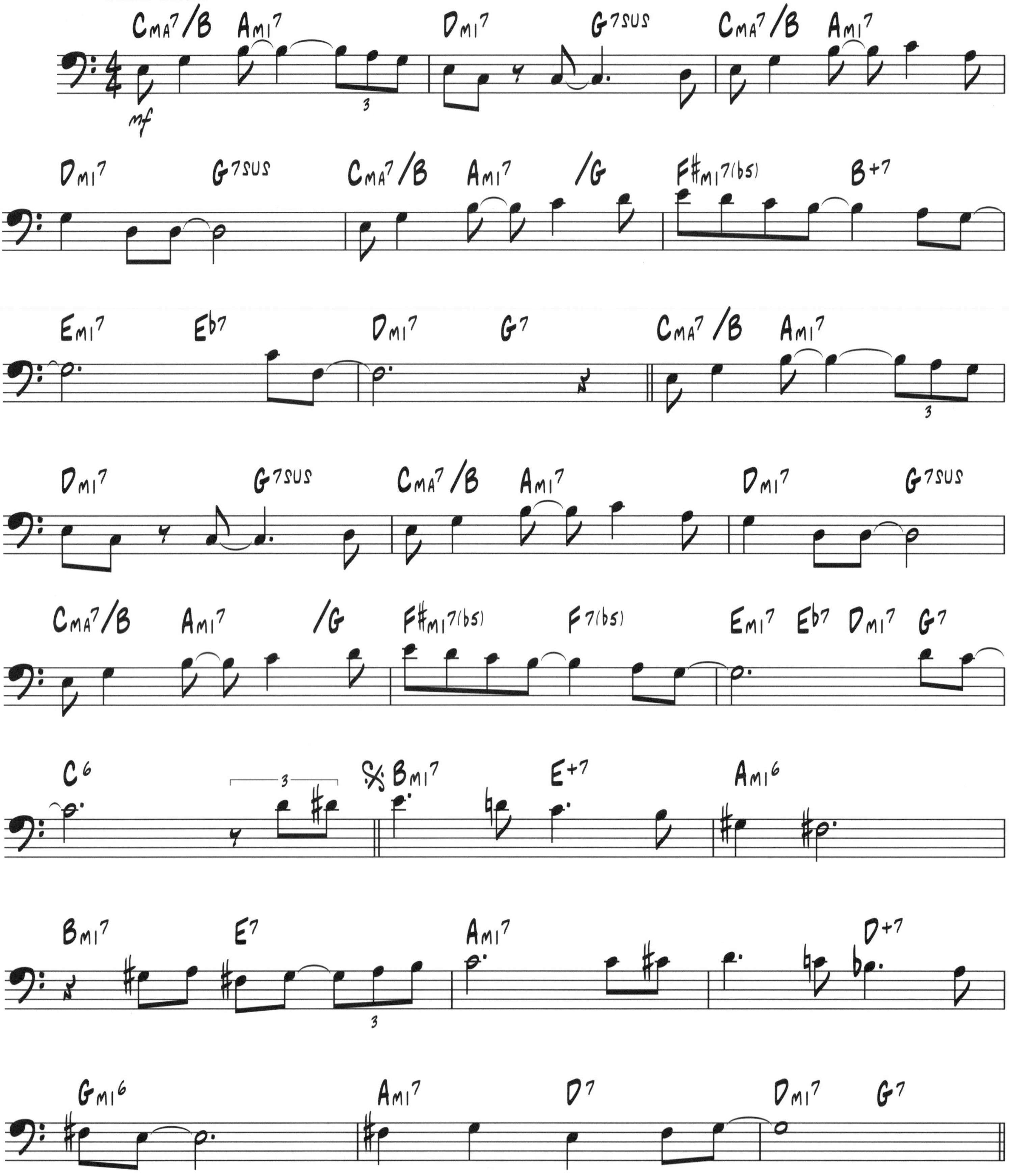
CMA7/B AMI7 DMI7 G7SUS CMA7/B AMI7
mf
3
DMI7 G7SUS CMA7/B AMI7 /G F#MI7(b5) B+7
EMI7 Eb7 DMI7 G7 CMA7/B AMI7
3
DMI7 G7SUS CMA7/B AMI7 DMI7 G7SUS
CMA7/B AMI7 /G F#MI7(b5) F7(b5) EMI7 Eb7 DMI7 G7
C6 BMI7 E+7 AMI6
3
BMI7 E7 AMI7 D+7
3
GMI6 AMI7 D7 DMI7 G7

CMA7/B AMI7 DMI7 G7SUS CMA7/B AMI7
DMI7 G7SUS CMA7/B AMI7 /G F#MI7(b5) F7(b5) TO CODA
EMI7 Eb7 DMI7 G7 C6 DbMA7
SOLO
CMA7 AMI7 DMI7 G7SUS CMA7 AMI7
DMI7 G7SUS CMA7 AMI7
1.
F#MI7(b5) B+7 EMI7 Eb7 DMI7 G7
2.
F#MI7(b5) F7(b5) EMI7 Eb7 DMI7 G7 C6 BMI7 E+7
AMI6 BMI7 E7 AMI7 D+7 GMI6
AMI7 D7(b9) DMI7 G7 CMA7 AMI7 DMI7 G7SUS CMA7 AMI7
D.S. AL CODA
DMI7 G7SUS CMA7 AMI7 F#MI7(b5) F7(b5) EMI7 Eb7 DMI7 G7 C6
CODA
EMI7 Eb7 DMI7 G7 Ab6 Bb6 C6
RIT.

CD #2

YOU ARE TOO BEAUTIFUL

FROM HALLELUJAH, I'M A BUM

WORDS BY LORENZ HART
MUSIC BY RICHARD RODGERS

C VERSION

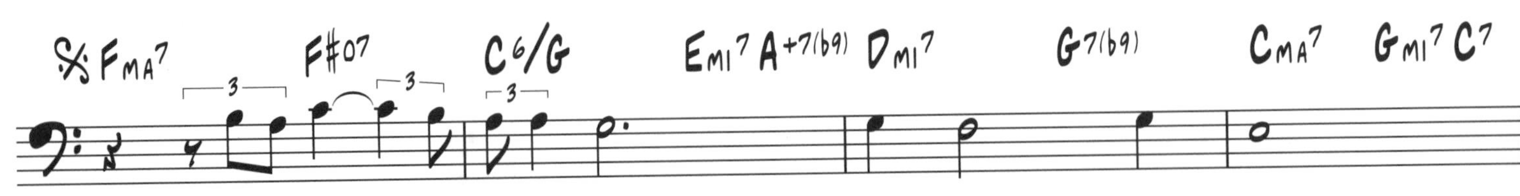

BMI7(b5) E7(b9) AMI7 D7SUS D7 Ab7(b5) G7 G7(b9)
F#MI7(b5) B+7(b9) EMI7 A+7(b9) DMI7 G+7(b9)
CMA7 GMI7 C7(b9) FMA7 Bb7 AMI7 D7SUS D7
TO CODA
SOLO
D7 D+7 G7SUS G7(b9) C6 EMI7 A+7(b9) F#MI7(b5) B+7(b9) EMI7 A+7(b9)
DMI7 G+7(b9) CMA7 GMI7 C7(b9) FMA7 Bb7 AMI7 D7SUS D7
1.
DMI7 G7(b9) EMI7 A+7(b9)
2.
D7 D+7 G7SUS G7(b9) C6
D.S. AL CODA
GMI7 C7
CODA
AbMA7 DbMA7 CMA7
RIT.

Presenting the Hal Leonard JAZZ PLAY-ALONG® SERIES

No.	Title	Item	Price
1.	DUKE ELLINGTON	00841644	$16.95
1A.	MAIDEN VOYAGE/ALL BLUES	00843158	$15.99
2.	MILES DAVIS	00841645	$16.95
3.	THE BLUES	00841646	$16.99
4.	JAZZ BALLADS	00841691	$16.99
5.	BEST OF BEBOP	00841689	$16.99
6.	JAZZ CLASSICS WITH EASY CHANGES	00841690	$16.99
7.	ESSENTIAL JAZZ STANDARDS	00843000	$16.99
8.	ANTONIO CARLOS JOBIM AND THE ART OF THE BOSSA NOVA	00843001	$16.95
9.	DIZZY GILLESPIE	00843002	$16.99
10.	DISNEY CLASSICS	00843003	$16.99
11.	RODGERS AND HART – FAVORITES	00843004	$16.99
12.	ESSENTIAL JAZZ CLASSICS	00843005	$16.99
13.	JOHN COLTRANE	00843006	$16.95
14.	IRVING BERLIN	00843007	$15.99
15.	RODGERS & HAMMERSTEIN	00843008	$15.99
16.	COLE PORTER	00843009	$15.95
17.	COUNT BASIE	00843010	$16.95
18.	HAROLD ARLEN	00843011	$15.95
19.	COOL JAZZ	00843012	$15.95
20.	CHRISTMAS CAROLS	00843080	$14.95
21.	RODGERS AND HART – CLASSICS	00843014	$14.95
22.	WAYNE SHORTER	00843015	$16.95
23.	LATIN JAZZ	00843016	$16.95
24.	EARLY JAZZ STANDARDS	00843017	$14.95
25.	CHRISTMAS JAZZ	00843018	$16.95
26.	CHARLIE PARKER	00843019	$16.95
27.	GREAT JAZZ STANDARDS	00843020	$15.99
28.	BIG BAND ERA	00843021	$15.99
29.	LENNON AND McCARTNEY	00843022	$16.95
30.	BLUES' BEST	00843023	$15.99
31.	JAZZ IN THREE	00843024	$15.99
32.	BEST OF SWING	00843025	$15.99
33.	SONNY ROLLINS	00843029	$15.95
34.	ALL TIME STANDARDS	00843030	$15.99
35.	BLUESY JAZZ	00843031	$15.99
36.	HORACE SILVER	00843032	$16.99
37.	BILL EVANS	00843033	$16.95
38.	YULETIDE JAZZ	00843034	$16.95
39.	"ALL THE THINGS YOU ARE" & MORE JEROME KERN SONGS	00843035	$15.99
40.	BOSSA NOVA	00843036	$15.99
41.	CLASSIC DUKE ELLINGTON	00843037	$16.99
42.	GERRY MULLIGAN – FAVORITES	00843038	$16.99
43.	GERRY MULLIGAN – CLASSICS	00843039	$16.95
44.	OLIVER NELSON	00843040	$16.95
45.	JAZZ AT THE MOVIES	00843041	$15.99
46.	BROADWAY JAZZ STANDARDS	00843042	$15.99
47.	CLASSIC JAZZ BALLADS	00843043	$15.99
48.	BEBOP CLASSICS	00843044	$16.99
49.	MILES DAVIS – STANDARDS	00843045	$16.95
50.	GREAT JAZZ CLASSICS	00843046	$15.99
51.	UP-TEMPO JAZZ	00843047	$15.99
52.	STEVIE WONDER	00843048	$15.95
53.	RHYTHM CHANGES	00843049	$15.99
54.	"MOONLIGHT IN VERMONT" & OTHER GREAT STANDARDS	00843050	$15.99
55.	BENNY GOLSON	00843052	$15.95
56.	"GEORGIA ON MY MIND" & OTHER SONGS BY HOAGY CARMICHAEL	00843056	$15.99
57.	VINCE GUARALDI	00843057	$16.99
58.	MORE LENNON AND McCARTNEY	00843059	$15.99
59.	SOUL JAZZ	00843060	$15.99
60.	DEXTER GORDON	00843061	$15.95
61.	MONGO SANTAMARIA	00843062	$15.95
62.	JAZZ-ROCK FUSION	00843063	$14.95
63.	CLASSICAL JAZZ	00843064	$14.95
64.	TV TUNES	00843065	$14.95
65.	SMOOTH JAZZ	00843066	$16.99
66.	A CHARLIE BROWN CHRISTMAS	00843067	$16.99
67.	CHICK COREA	00843068	$15.95
68.	CHARLES MINGUS	00843069	$16.95
69.	CLASSIC JAZZ	00843071	$15.99
70.	THE DOORS	00843072	$14.95
71.	COLE PORTER CLASSICS	00843073	$14.95
72.	CLASSIC JAZZ BALLADS	00843074	$15.99
73.	JAZZ/BLUES	00843075	$14.95
74.	BEST JAZZ CLASSICS	00843076	$15.99
75.	PAUL DESMOND	00843077	$14.95
76.	BROADWAY JAZZ BALLADS	00843078	$15.99
77.	JAZZ ON BROADWAY	00843079	$15.99
78.	STEELY DAN	00843070	$14.99
79.	MILES DAVIS – CLASSICS	00843081	$15.99
80.	JIMI HENDRIX	00843083	$15.99
81.	FRANK SINATRA – CLASSICS	00843084	$15.99
82.	FRANK SINATRA – STANDARDS	00843085	$15.99
83.	ANDREW LLOYD WEBBER	00843104	$14.95
84.	BOSSA NOVA CLASSICS	00843105	$14.95
85.	MOTOWN HITS	00843109	$14.95
86.	BENNY GOODMAN	00843110	$14.95
87.	DIXIELAND	00843111	$14.95
88.	DUKE ELLINGTON FAVORITES	00843112	$14.95
89.	IRVING BERLIN FAVORITES	00843113	$14.95
90.	THELONIOUS MONK CLASSICS	00841262	$16.99
91.	THELONIOUS MONK FAVORITES	00841263	$16.99
92.	LEONARD BERNSTEIN	00450134	$15.99
93.	DISNEY FAVORITES	00843142	$14.99
94.	RAY	00843143	$14.99
95.	JAZZ AT THE LOUNGE	00843144	$14.99
96.	LATIN JAZZ STANDARDS	00843145	$14.99
97.	MAYBE I'M AMAZED	00843148	$15.99
98.	DAVE FRISHBERG	00843149	$15.99
99.	SWINGING STANDARDS	00843150	$14.99
100.	LOUIS ARMSTRONG	00740423	$15.99
101.	BUD POWELL	00843152	$14.99
102.	JAZZ POP	00843153	$14.99
103.	ON GREEN DOLPHIN STREET & OTHER JAZZ CLASSICS	00843154	$14.99
104.	ELTON JOHN	00843155	$14.99
105.	SOULFUL JAZZ	00843151	$15.99
106.	SLO' JAZZ	00843117	$14.99
107.	MOTOWN CLASSICS	00843116	$14.99
108.	JAZZ WALTZ	00843159	$15.99
109.	OSCAR PETERSON	00843160	$15.99
110.	JUST STANDARDS	00843161	$15.99
111.	COOL CHRISTMAS	00843162	$15.99
114.	MODERN JAZZ QUARTET FAVORITES	00843163	$15.99
115.	THE SOUND OF MUSIC	00843164	$15.99
116.	JACO PASTORIUS	00843165	$15.99
117.	ANTONIO CARLOS JOBIM – MORE HITS	00843166	$15.99
118.	BIG JAZZ STANDARDS COLLECTION	00843167	$27.50
119.	JELLY ROLL MORTON	00843168	$15.99
120.	J.S. BACH	00843169	$15.99
121.	DJANGO REINHARDT	00843170	$15.99
122.	PAUL SIMON	00843182	$16.99
123.	BACHARACH & DAVID	00843185	$15.99
124.	JAZZ-ROCK HORN HITS	00843186	$15.99
126.	COUNT BASIE CLASSICS	00843157	$15.99

Prices, contents, and availability subject to change without notice.

For More Information, See Your Local Music Dealer, Or Write To:

HAL•LEONARD®
CORPORATION
7777 W. Bluemound Rd. P.O. Box 13819
Milwaukee, Wisconsin 53213

Visit Hal Leonard online at
www.halleonard.com
for complete songlists.

0910